HAVE FAITH *without* FEAR

HAVE FAITH
without FEAR

Kenneth L. Wilson

1817

HARPER & ROW, PUBLISHERS

NEW YORK, EVANSTON, AND LONDON

Contents

I am grateful to Christian Herald *magazine, in which most of my ideas originally appeared, for permission to revise and expand them into a book. Special thanks are due also to the Adult Fellowship Class of First Baptist Church, White Plains, New York, whose members have been on the receiving and challenging end of such thoughts as these for the ten years I have been their teacher and they mine.*

HAVE FAITH *without* FEAR

To the reader

Writing a book is a presumption, any way you look at it. The writer must assume either that what he is about to commit to paper will be of absorbing interest to the reader, or that his thoughts and conclusions (if anything can indeed be concluded, even thoughts) are worth sharing. With as little presumption as possible, I will try to tell how things look to me. The humbling question is whether what I see and think matters in the slightest. But that is what readers are for. They, motivated by the same drives that motivate authors, are the jurors. Unless they share the task of authorship, unless they authenticate the book out of their own reactions to it, there is no book. It takes not only a writer, but a reader to make a book.

So the question is not only what I think, but what you think as you read. If something here and there makes you feel more alive, more adequate, more at home in God's living room—which is to say, the world—my thoughts and yours will be healing and creative ones.

For so many decades we were told what we "had to" believe. In recent years we have been told what we were not to believe. At the point where the bunking and debunking have left us, let us together try to discover what it is that authenticates itself to us, that provides a basis of Christian belief so credible, so joyous, so *natural* that our faith won't have to be drummed up, only discovered and used.

1) Getting the heaven scared out of us

There are many scared Christians today—Christians with no need to be scared. The Christian faith and fear simply don't go together, contrary to what has been drilled into us by cheerless believers who go through life as if they were walking on eggs— rotten eggs at that. One will indeed encounter eggs here and there, perhaps even some overaged ones, but there comes a point at which anxiety ceases to be productive and becomes counterproductive. No matter how cautious one is, either the eggs are going to break or they aren't. Besides, faith has something to do with coping with broken eggs.

As a veteran egg-walker, I know what it's like. I know how it feels to be boxed in by one's faith, restricted, constricted. And I know the agony of liberation and then the wonderment when liberation is accomplished and one discovers and recovers the faith that God's wide, great, wonderful world is out there waiting and that one doesn't have to be afraid of it. Being "born again" is the dramatic way Jesus referred to this breakthrough. For me the discovery wasn't a matter of going from no faith to faith, but from a fear-dominated faith to one liberated from fear.

The Bible is a liberating book. The tragedy is that it has been made part of the apparatus of fear. Some still think the proper treatment of a sinner is to "throw the Book at him."

Theology, which ought to be the way to describe the joy of opening wide one's arms to a boundless sky, has become a well-ordered wall of small apothecary drawers, each carefully labeled and crossindexed, holding precisely defined and inviolable concepts. Nothing throws an apothecary-drawer Christian into more confusion than being handed a new idea that won't quite fit into one of the drawers. Either he has to discard an old idea to make room for a new one, a process that is strenuously resisted; or the new idea is discarded, which is the easiest solution; or the new idea is reluctantly accommodated.

My "theology," if that is the word for it, is not systematic. I'm more interested in the *theo* (God) part than in the *logy* (system) part. Some of the thoughts that impress me and perhaps you may be contradictory. Or, an idea that strikes me today may be different from one that struck me last week, or that will confront me next week. Some ideas may offer a clue in one setting and not in another. But none of this bothers me any more. The "whole truth" is an unreasonable expectation and an impossible demand. I've decided that truth comes in bits and pieces, and that if one piece seems not to fit against another, it may be simply because there are missing pieces that belong in between.

There is another thought that can either dismay or comfort us, and I choose to be comforted by it: the impossibility inherent in our seeking. We're forever hunting what we can never really find. For what we finite types are trying to do is to define the infinite, to say the unsayable. When you reconcile yourself to that, you immediately become more tolerant of the other person's definitions or statements of belief. So if the man in the next pew wants to say that the streets of heaven are paved with gold, I don't quarrel with him, though gold doesn't strike me as being as adequate a paving material as some others, and this isn't the way I would try to express the unsayable concept of heaven. I'm not sure that I would even talk about streets. Or think of heaven as a place with a zip code. Or be very concerned about heaven at all, for that matter.

None of this seems to me to fall under the heading of losing my faith. Rather, it seems to me to fall under the heading of finding it, for faith is the evidence of things not seen, confidence in contemplation of the unseeable and the inexpressible. To contemplate, I have to translate ideas into words and pictures my own mind's eye can see and my own experience can grasp. Jesus recognized the problem: "The Kingdom of heaven is *like unto.* . . ."

Is it indeed possible to have faith without fear? Does not the

Bible say, "The fear of the Lord is the beginning of wisdom"? Therefore, isn't fear a good, robust, healthful thing to have?

This brings us back to the point that the Bible is a liberating book and that fear is one thing from which it liberates. The road between biblical advocacy of fear to the bald and equally biblical statement that "perfect love casts out fear" is a long, difficult trail littered with the bones of saints. Our love is not perfect. But love and fear cannot occupy the same ground. There may be some of one and some of the other. But the more there is of one, the less there is of the other.

If the fear of the Lord is the beginning of wisdom, the perfect love of the Lord is surely the end of wisdom. Can we assume that though we may not yet be at the end, we are, most of us, a step or two beyond beginnings?

2) Fear goes with not knowing

But perhaps we are not much more than a step beyond beginnings. We are afraid of our shadows. And what is a shadow but a by-product of light? The only way not to cast a shadow is to live a gray life in a gray world, a life-style at which many Christians have become adept.

But it is not only shadows we fear. We are afraid of new light, which is to say new ideas, new experiences, change. We are afraid because we don't know what to expect. The familiar is always passing away.

Sometimes I think if we had our way, we would tell God exactly what he could and couldn't do, so that we wouldn't be caught by surprise.

We would tartly inform him that he lives in church, not just any old where.

That Sunday is a holier day than any other and that while he may have appointments on other days, it's to be understood that his office hours are Sunday, 11 A.M. to noon.

That when anything "religious" happens he is to see to it that it happens through approved channels.

That the Bible is the Constitution of the universe, and he's not to do anything that's unconstitutional. No 29th chapter of Acts, please.

But God is not about to be told what he may or can do and may not or can't do. He keeps breaking out all over. No sooner do we accept the possibility that he can appear in a burning bush, than he speaks from a burning city and we say, "Back to the bush!" It was hard enough getting used to the bush, and now the change in setting really confuses and frightens us. It catches us off guard. We thought we had things all figured out, then something happens that doesn't fit.

Fear goes with not being able to explain something, with not knowing. Thus it would seem, would it not, that those who know God best should be least afraid—of anything? But this isn't always the way it works. The way it often works is that we confuse knowing God with containing God, imprisoning him in a concept that gives us a sense of security. He's safely "there" when we want to peek through a Gothic arch at him, not loose somewhere wreaking havoc with our carefully worked-out notions. When he breaks out, despite our best efforts, we think we have "lost" him. One could as well lose the universe!

Perhaps the problem is simply that we don't recognize him when we see him somewhere else.

There is something pathetic in even the scriptural stories of high moments of religious inspiration. Consider the birth of Jesus. Before the angel—and let us not get hung up on angels at this point—could tell the "good tidings of great joy," he had to allay the fears of the hearers: "Be not afraid." Talk about irony! Humanity cowering on the threshold of good news! The same at the resurrection. How many times must the Master say, in Scripture or out, "It is I, be not afraid"? Apparently every time we find him out of the place or image we have assigned to him!

Could it be that we don't recognize the Lord simply because we don't know him very well?

At Kennedy airport one evening, I was looking for the Pan Am representative who was to take a small group of editors to South America. I had to find him because he had my ticket. I had met him just once before, and wasn't sure I would know him when I saw him. I took a seat in the nearby waiting area and studied each person who approached the check-in counter. Was that Mr. Dreslin? Did he look like that? Did he walk like that? No. How about that other man just coming in? No, that couldn't be he. Finally, I singled him out, heaved a sigh of relief, and went over to collect my ticket and check my bags.

A week or so before I had been waiting in Grand Central Station for my wife, who was arriving on the 6:05. We were on our once-a-year binge—dinner in New York and a play. From my favorite waiting spot at the information booth under the clock, I looked across the big room toward the gate from which she would enter. Presently the passengers began streaming in from the 6:05. The moment she walked through the gate I knew who it was, though I had only a flashing glimpse of her. I didn't need to conduct a detailed study of all comers. I didn't need to look for somebody wearing gray-rimmed glasses or a pin with the Chinese character that means "long life." I knew her so well that I could identify her with a fleeting glance. Smiling, she came toward the information booth, for she had spotted me, too.

Do we know God well enough to recognize him in a voice, a word, an act of impetuous compassion, a commitment, a life-style? When we do not, we are discommoded, nervous, fearful. Recognizing him in unanticipated places requires a new life-style of our own, an openness to new ideas, a sense of the worth and integrity of personhood.

Adjusting to change is probably the most difficult adjustment of all. And yet, change is the mark of aliveness. We sing, "Change and decay in all around I see, O thou who changest not, abide with me."

We might better say, "Change *or* decay," for only when the process
of change ceases can decay set in. Dr. David Thaeler, staff physician
at a retirement community in Penney Farms, Florida, and himself
past retirement age, showed me a set of four-inch-thick manuals
through which he was working his way in his spare time. It was an
advanced electronics course. Already a "ham" radio operator, the
course he was now taking was one that would qualify him for an
FCC commercial license in television engineering—a post he never
expected to hold nor wished to hold. "The course stretches my mind,"
he said. "It's hard. I have to think. Only when a person stops thinking
hard, does his thinking ability diminish."

Decay is a part of God's order too. Decay is itself a part of continuing life and represents the ultimate contribution to life to come.
But it's a contribution we shouldn't be impatient to make. "Heaven is
my home," a lively senior citizen once said, "but I'm not homesick."

As to God's unchangingness, even that might be debated, but we
really haven't had enough time to research the topic. How many years
of written history do we have on the shelves—6,000, 10,000? Out
of a few million years, or timelessness for that matter, we have a very
small slice, indeed.

Anyway, the song says, "O thou who changest not, abide with
me," not, "Let me who changest not, abide with thee."

If we fear change—pathologically, acutely fear it—we will never
feel at home in life.

3) We're forever
playing "Statue"

It was great fun, when we were little. For most of us, in some
way or other, it still is. You remember how the game went. It was

spontaneous and unrehearsed, the kind of thing that just happened on a warm summer evening. On our street, the game usually began after the big arc light at the corner of Clayton and University avenues came on and we were trying to think of reasons why it wasn't yet time to go to that despised and inescapable fate of childhood—bed. I was more fortunate than many small boys today, for my life was blessed with many of the incomparable advantages that adults look upon as hardships. For one thing, we lived on an unpaved street, where, from a boy's point of view, the dust blew in great beautiful clouds and the rain ran off in unchanneled torrents of water and mud that only bare feet could properly appreciate. For another thing, we—like most Pittsburghers—lived on a hill. To adults this meant climbing up or down long hillside wooden stairways. To a boy a hill meant a place from which to contemplate a wonderland of city lights, rivers, bridges, and other hills.

Our street-light corner had grass-grown vacant lots and fields on three sides. One belonged to an orphanage, another to the one-time "manor house" of the neighborhood where there was also a garden and four or five pear trees whose fruit no boy had patience enough to allow to ripen. (To this day I am always pleasantly surprised to find that pears sold in stores are sweet and yellow instead of rock-hard and green.) Our parents, I am sure, regarded the grassy open spaces as weedy and altogether unkempt, even though a spry old retired preacher dearly loved by the children cut the grass on the manor-house side with a scythe when it reached knee-height. The deeper the grass the better we liked it, for then you could roll and fall without getting hurt. Rolling and falling were very important in the game of "Statue."

There wasn't much to it, really. Somebody who was "it" took each of the others one at a time by the arm, swung him or her and let go in a kind of hammer throw. The person would then freeze in whatever position he or she landed. I'm somewhat hazy about the rules from that point on, but I think the object was to see who could hold a frozen pose the longest. The moment you altered position, even to the crook of a finger, you were "out."

All this may seem to be a long-winded way of getting to the point. But the temptation to reminisce is perhaps itself the point: I find it easy to do now what I did then—to play "Statue," to freeze a particular moment or period of history into a forever-inviolate, forever-solidified image. We are all doing it all the time, and some of the ways in which we do it stifle our growth as persons. As soon as we freeze a particular moment, a particular idea, a particular dogma, into a this-is-*it* finality, we in effect stop the clock. Then the object of the game, as we play it, is to see who can maintain his position the longest. To deviate in the slightest is to be read out of whatever group happens to be playing the game.

One interesting thing about all this is that each of the ideas we so willingly freeze, itself supplants some other idea that somebody else once froze. One of the best examples of this has been church architecture. Anyone who has ever been a member of a church involved in a building project has heard some other member say disparagingly of some building which has been brought to the congregation's attention, "It doesn't look like a church!" What this usually boils down to is that it doesn't look like a Gothic church structure. Yet, when the Gothic style was introduced, exactly the same thing was said about it. Even the name given it—Gothic— was a shuddering epithet, for the Goths were the barbarians of their day. Somebody obviously did some unfreezing somewhere along the way. Today some are unfreezing even more, for now the question is not so much architectural style as it is the validity of the church-in-a-building concept versus the church-in-the-world concept.

Memorial Day is another example of memory-freezing in action, and a cemetery is not by happenstance a place of many statues. Memory's eye stopped the action at some specific point. Perhaps it was at the best point, perhaps the worst. When we think of this or that lamented one with whom once we talked and laughed and perhaps quarreled, we don't think of the whole person but of the person he was at the moment our judgment clamped down upon him to make him eternally better or worse than he was.

The small briskly waving flags that mark military graves conjure

up visions of smart uniforms and muffled drums, rather than of men who were young and who were old, who lived with hope or with hopelessness, who loved and were loved, who were confident and who were frightened, who found it no easier to die than the rest of us. When we stop the action, play "Statue," there is so much of a man or an idea we have to leave out.

To play "Statue" with even our social and religious documents is to say that we were wiser at one stage in our human history than we expect ever to be again, and that there is nothing more to be learned about some reverently frozen topics than what we have already learned. We tend to feel this way, for example, about the U.S. Constitution. It is indeed one of the great documents of all time and serves us well; the men who shaped it were indeed wise men. At the same time, twenty-five amendments to the Constitution give notice that its framers were not *all-wise* except to the extent they made provision for amendments to patch gaps in their far-sightedness. The writers of the Constitution obviously recognized that they had not said the last word, and that, indeed, no one ever could. This does not diminish them or it, but elevates both. It is the unfrozenness of the Constitution that makes it and keeps it a living force. May it be that a man or a document is infallible only to the extent that he or it admits to fallibility?

How easy it is for us to play "Statue"—to generalize the specific, to universalize the local, to eternalize the split second. When something works for us, makes sense to us, is beneficial to us, we immediately have the urge to embalm it, though there is no surer way to defeat our own good purposes. The earliest automobiles—which were little more than motorized buggies—were built with whip sockets, even though there were no whips and nothing to whip. We still tend to call the instrument panel a dashboard because that is what the front end of a buggy used to be called. In many colleges today endowment funds are lying idle because they were restricted to the teaching of subjects no one any longer wants to learn. Somebody was playing "Statue," trying to make sure that something that once seemed important would always be important.

Some of the early settlers who came to America to achieve religious freedom promptly imprisoned everyone else in their concept of religious freedom. The woods were full of people playing "Statue," and they still are, people who say, "You are free to believe as I believe."

While we play "Statue" in our various ways, the world keeps on the move. We may stop our clock, but other clocks will go on. The longer and the deeper the freeze, the harder it is to catch up. Scientists tell us that ailing human bodies may someday be literally frozen and stored against the time when there is a cure for their disease or when somebody feels like bringing them out of cold storage—"cryogenics" is the word for it. But to revive a person in fifty or a hundred years would be to thrust him into an environment for which he was utterly unprepared. For him, the world could be a baffling hell. He would have to learn all over again how to exist, for his points of reference would be gone—as many of them are gone for us, over even a twenty- or thirty-year span. The difference for us is that we have, more or less, kept up.

I sometimes wonder about my father, who died only thirty years ago, and who sometimes pitched quoits on one of those grass-grown lots while I played, and who built with such pride one of the first crystal radio sets in our neighborhood. I wonder how he would react, if he could suddenly look in today? He never saw television. He always wanted to ride in a plane but never did. He never owned a car or rode a superhighway or shopped in a supermarket or met his grandchildren. I think he would love life today—though, of course, Dad was an exception. But there I am, playing "Statue" myself.

Taking up residence in the present tense is not as easy as it looks. When we get dewy-eyed about the past, we romanticize everyone who lived there. They were real people, and their doubts were not resolved for them any more easily than ours for us.

Take, to pick up a couple of years, 1776 and A.D. 33.

4) The revolution once delivered

Ask almost anyone what he regards as the high-water mark of American patriotism and the answer you likely will get is July 4, 1776. When we think of July 4 we think of the American Revolution, and the thought becomes suffused with a misty, nostalgic, evangelistic fervor. This seems to happen to some people more noticeably than to others. I get the feeling that it happens most noticeably in the most unrevolutionary people. You would think that if the mere word "revolution" today sends someone into spasms of dismay, he would be no friend of any revolution anywhere at any time. But as nearly as I can tell, that isn't the way it works.

It causes me to wonder. When I hear the speech-making on the Fourth of July, and at other times and places see angelic and utterly proper souls denouncing revolution in the name of Revolution, I can't help wondering what they would have done if they had been there. Whose side would they have been on?

I'm not even so sure about myself, for basically I'm a non-revolutionary type. Where would I have been during the Boston Tea Party? Probably calling the cops. Probably defending the sacred rights of property, especially if I owned a home, as I do now, and had a wife and children, as I have. "Stay away from the water!" I would have warned the kids. "Those demonstrators at the harbor are up to no good and they'll get you into trouble."

When Paul Revere clattered by, yelling, "The British are coming!" I might have taken a reassuring look at the verse in the Bible which says, "All authority is ordained of God," and yelled back, "Thank God, they're finally coming!" I just don't know.

And frankly, I just don't know how some of today's judgmental super-patriots would have behaved then, either. On the basis of how they behave now, I think they would have regarded the defenders of freedom then as a rag-taggle lot, and would themselves have been in sympathy with the Establishment. But with our 20/20 hindsight, when we talk about British sympathizers it is with disdain and even incomprehension that there could have been any.

Now, I am not trying to incite anyone to revolution. I'm simply calling attention to the fact that at least once in this country the revolutionaries turned out to be the good guys. This is awfully easy to forget, for the past tense makes the heart grow fonder. The uncomfortable truth is that a lot of us who have happily enjoyed life produced by revolution in this nation wouldn't have been caught dead in the Revolution itself. And yet in the name of 200-year-old patriotic dissent, they want to make present patriotic dissent a crime punishable by death or worse.

If a revolutionary is not without honor save in his own decade, the same goes for a prophet. Being a prophet looks like a pretty good thing, once you get him safely enshrined in the pages of the Bible. What we forget is that the prophets themselves were not safely enshrined. They were right out in the open, the most exposed men of their times. You can't be a prophet without saying what you think, and this invariably upsets your contemporaries. You never heard of a diplomatic prophet. You never heard of an on-beat prophet. You never heard of a popular prophet, except the false ones who weren't prophets at all but were simply clever at telling people what they wanted to hear.

Today we love the prophets—the biblical ones, that is—but if we had been there, I wonder. Who wants an Amos calling "Foul!" every time we shade just a bit on our income-tax return, and yelling it loud enough for everyone to hear? Who wants a Jeremiah predicting that the enemy is going to win? As for Hosea, he couldn't keep his own wife straight. And John the Baptist couldn't even keep himself straight. He was a sloppy dresser, ate any old thing, wouldn't work at a respectable job, and lived out among the rocks somewhere.

Would you have wanted your daughter to marry John the Baptist? Personally, I wouldn't even have wanted him on my living-room sofa.

But he and other beatniks of the Bible look quite respectable from today's germ-free distance. We've shifted to targets closer at hand. We're outraged now by the very same outspoken, piercing-eye, unconventional performance that we have learned to respect in those other men who have been deodorized by time. Of course, long hair does not a prophet make, or unwashed clothes a saint. There are phonies now just as there were phonies then. But probably the major test of prophethood is about the same in any era: the real ones are those who make us uncomfortable. And the only way you can really make people uncomfortable is to question their values. Am I putting my priorities in the wrong places? If you can make me wonder that about myself, you shake me up, and I don't like to be shaken any more than the next person.

So the validity of the prophet may depend more upon me than upon him. If he shakes me—if I let him shake me—he's a prophet. If he doesn't, if I don't, he isn't. Judging by the jerry-built regulations being thrown together to cope with everything from hair-styling and draft-card burning to how tight pants cuffs can be or what length skirt is decent, it's clear that a lot of people are being shaken one way or another.

I am making no effort to incite this sort of revolution, either, but simply am indicating that we may hallow at long range what we often can't stand close up and in person. The issue is always treason —treason to country, to manners, to customs, to beliefs. But, given enough time, one man's treason may become another man's patriotism. And you can find any number of religious reformations that should remind us that one man's heresy may become another man's faith.

But it's hard for us to see over the tops of our preconceptions. We've made "prophecy" into a favorite speculative topic, when it was in fact the raw edge of reality, of relevance, of the contemporary. The topics that hurt to talk about, the controversial, the troublemaking—that was prophecy. Prophecy was that which was most immediately important. It was what was *now*. It was where the action was. The paradox today is that "prophecy" has so little to do with what *is* happening, only about what somebody said *was* happening centuries ago or what may happen centuries hence— just about as substantial a job of table-turning as you're likely to find anywhere. When somebody today dares to say something about the immediate in the name of God, he is promptly told that this is none of the church's business. Let the church have full jurisdiction over any tense but the present, cry today's stoners of the prophets.

I am not sure beyond a reasonable doubt how I would have behaved when the guards led a young bearded religious dissenter before the judgment seat of Pilate. As far as the respectable element of the town was concerned, here was a man who had nothing going for him. He owned no property, had no regular mailing address, had no visible source of income, made people uneasy by what he said and did, appealed primarily to the disadvantaged. I would like to think that I would have been more discerning, had I been there, than the scribes who were. I would like to think I would not have taken up the chant, "Crucify him!" But I wonder. And how do you suppose those church members who are so rooted and grounded that they're practically sprouting would have accepted the open challenge of their most untouchable religious traditions, when today they go into shock if the pastor shifts the *Doxology* from after the offering to before the offering?

I have the feeling that we can't separate the patriots from the prophets easily, and perhaps not at all. They belong together.

But if we need to be able to live today without fear, the same goes for tomorrow. What will happen then? Where are we going?

5) Getting from here to where

There is something about stepping-stones that dares you to go where they will take you. The water between them may be swift-flowing. Some of the stones will offer less than solid footing while some will be as secure as Gibraltar—and you won't know which are which until you leap. That's the way of stepping-stones, and of life itself.

You see all kinds of people on stepping-stones. There's one in every crowd who loses his balance and gets wet feet or worse. There's the timid soul who makes it to the first or second stone and then cowers there, arms wildly gyrating, trying to decide what to do next. There's the blithe and sometimes reckless spirit who leaps sure-footed as a mountain goat from stone to stone. And then there are the rest of us, moving along cautiously or even gingerly, but moving, and at our wobbliest not when we are moving but when we are not moving.

Stepping-stones are, for most people in most situations, like eating potato chips: you can't stop with one. But for others, stopping with one or two or three is not only a possibility but their normal way of life. For you can divide stepping-stones of whatever category into three classifications: the ones you have already stood upon; the one you now stand upon; and the ones you have not yet stood upon. To put it another way: there's where you have been; there's where you are; there's where you may someday be if you've got the divine inquisitiveness it takes to get there.

The blithe and reckless leapers we won't worry much about here. They not only do not welcome our solicitude, but a wet foot now and then doesn't seem to bother them and only adds to their general excitement.

The timid soul we probably can't do much about, either. Certainly the surest way to cause him to lose his footing is to drag him screaming to the next stone, and it's a good way to lose your own equilibrium in the bargain. Stepping-stones are something you have to tackle by yourself, for yourself. You can't push or pull somebody along. You can urge him on, talk him on, cheer him on, but that's about it. Anyway, don't think he's got to stand on your stone just because *you're* there; on a stepping-stone, there's very little room for company.

So that leaves the rest of us, torn between daring and timidity, between the *status quo* and the *status go*, between dynamism and dogma, between open-endedness and closed-mindedness. What can we do about us? What can I do about me?

Well, right off I can see a couple of examples that I don't want to emulate. I don't want to embalm the past, or even the present, which, as we have seen, is exactly the inclination of so many of the people moving through life. When they get something that they like, that they believe, they stop the action, build a roof over it and a shrine around it and live there happily ever after. When they find a stepping-stone to their liking, they floodlight it, decorate it, reinforce it with concrete, as if they expected to stay there forever. We have a talent for making stepping-stones into cornerstones. But stepping-stones were never meant to be lived on; it's standing room only.

But if I don't intend to embalm the past, neither do I care to "bomb" it. After all, it brought me to where I am. It's not superfluous because it's old any more than it's sacred because it's old. One can have respect for tradition without being imprisoned by it. Though you don't take up housekeeping on every stepping-stone as you come to it, neither do you pretend, after you're safely past, that it didn't matter.

Even if one agrees that all truth is tentative—as apparently Paul did when he wrote, ". . . whether there be knowledge, it shall vanish away . . . now I know in part . . ."—this doesn't mean that all, or any, truth is unimportant. And actually, the most important stepping-stone of the whole string for me is the one I am standing upon at this very moment. It is carrying my weight. It is holding me up. It is keeping me above water.

No man's faith, no child's faith, is to be despised. At this moment, it's the most important faith he's got. It may change. The child will grow and put away childish things, religious and otherwise. The man, too, will think and rethink as long as he continues to grow in mind and spirit. But right now, both must have a place to stand. Archimedes, an early physicist and quite a man with levers, is reputed to have said, "Give me a place to stand and I will move the earth!" The trouble now is that a lot of the people trying to move the world don't have any place to stand. They've scoffed at every foundation of faith, at every basis of belief.

There's more truth to come—how can anyone *not* believe this? But it's not here yet and we're not there yet. In the meantime, we must have a place to stand, and the one immediate stepping-stone is it. From there I will go on to something else, unless I convince myself that the last word has been spoken, the last truth uncovered.

I've seen too many convinced people in too many periods of history, to buy that. Knowledge is strewn with stepping-stones, each of which somebody thought was the end of the line.

You see clearly the stepping-stones in invention. Once there was a man by the name of Marconi, and he found out how to make a wireless set, using a spark coil and I don't know what else. Then came a man named Lee DeForrest, who invented the vacuum tube that opened up the whole field of electronics and made possible early radio transmission. Back about 1923 in Pittsburgh, people were building crystal sets like mad, to receive not only the local station, KDKA, but distant places. My father announced one morning, after a night's session of crouching under his headphones and tinkering with what he called a cat's whisker, "I brought in Schenectady last night!" Schenectady! What was the world coming to?

Then vacuum tubes replaced the galena detector, and a loud-speaker the headphones, and then television pushed the radio to one side. Then the transistor replaced the vacuum tube, and this was followed by miniaturization and micro-miniaturization. One stepping-stone after another, and each time only the next step was faintly visible. Each time, there was the temptation to settle down, thinking we had discovered just about all there was to discover.

Now we hear talk of holographic laser projection. Visualize a man in a room in New York talking to a man sitting in another chair in that room. The first man can walk around the second man, talk to him, see him from all sides, hear him speak—but that second man isn't there: he's in Miami. It will all be done with laser, which I don't pretend to understand. I never even understood how a cat's whisker worked!

Who has the arrogance to "bomb" one link out of that kind of chain? Or any other kind, whether of our national identity or our faith? Which stone would you dispense with? I don't want to "bomb" any of them. Neither do I want to embalm any of them. I'm glad I'm where I am, and I hope to have the courage to follow the stones of truth wherever they lead, even when I do not know where they will lead, which will usually be the case. But this much I know and will know: they will somehow lead to God, who *is* Truth.

When missionary Lillian Dickson first received parcels of used Christmas cards in Formosa, the post office clerk told her she would have to pay duty. "But they have no commercial value!" she said.

"Duty!" he insisted.

In despair she asked her friend K. C. Wu, the governor, to write a letter to the clerk explaining the facts of life about old Christmas cards. When a suitable time had elapsed, she returned to the post office. The clerk saw her coming and took out the letter from his desk and reread it silently, while she waited. He read it a second time, trying to find some way to save face. A third time he read it, then looked triumphantly over the top of his glasses.

"It doesn't say forever!" he announced.

Write that one on your stepping-stone. "It doesn't say forever!" And write it on the next one. And the next one.

But write something else, too, as, truth-driven, you go on and on into the unknown as far as your thoughts and your faith and your hope and your love will carry you. Write what another Pittsburgher, John Alfred Brashear, lensmaker and astronomer, wrote for his final stepping-stone, the one that lies over the place where he and his wife are buried: "We have loved the stars too fondly to be fearful of the night."

With that kind of fear out of the way—fear of what is out there at the next stepping-stone or around the next bend in the road or under the next leaf of the calendar—we're just about ready to start living. For it's not all out there ahead somewhere. If we're going to live, now is where we shall have to do it. For one thing—as of this moment, now is all we've got.

6) Putting your weight down, for pleasure and profit

For a few years there, we were hearing about sit-ins, lie-ins, pray-ins, teach-ins, and of course there were always break-ins and stand-ins. The sit-in goes back many years to a strike in a Detroit auto plant, as I recall, but then they called it a sit-down. Some of the other terms are old, some are new. There appears to be room in the "ins" for almost anything anyone wishes to do or not do. The be-in, more or less a latecomer, was a summer phenomenon that took place mostly in parks and required nothing much but massive thereness.

Be-ins were one of the antics of the hippies, those disturbed and disturbing youngsters who tried to resign from the human race because they felt that things were getting out of hand and because they had the notion that anybody over thirty was a hypocrite. But there were and are also such things as hippiecrites. There is an inescapable phoniness in expecting that society will somehow provide bread earned by the sweat of other men's brows to those whose brows are not only unfurrowed but amazingly unheated. Flower-power has its place, but somebody needs to make a speech about the tremendously important place of flour-power in the world.

But their be-ins taught us one thing, and that was the right name for a life-transforming technique we've historically neglected and often scorned. Bare feet aside, the be-in philosophy is not only a good one for anybody to practice, but is an essential one and perhaps the essential one for Christians to practice. It has nothing to do with the trappings of living, but with one's degree of aliveness. It has a great deal to do with confidence, with enjoyment, with total submersion. This kind of be-in is what the Sermon on the Mount is all about, what the story of the Good Samaritan is all about. It means awareness, awakeness. It means at-home-ness in life.

Some Christians seem never to feel altogether at ease about being alive. They act a little apologetic about the whole thing. If they happen to enjoy something, they remember that nasty word "hedonism" and promptly think about something unpleasant to take away the sweet taste in their mouths. They don't trust life. They feel that it's out to get them. They glibly recite John 3:16, though they despise this world God loved and loves still. So they have to be preoccupied with some other world. And that's too bad, because here is where they are.

The pity is that if you're preoccupied, you never quite know what's going on. There is a certain transferable wry truth in the pathetic characterization, "not all there." *Thereness* is the key to a victorious and radiant Christian style of living.

I don't know how it is with you, but I run into a lot of people who seem to have their minds on something else while I'm talking with them. I have the feeling they would rather be talking to someone else, doing something else. They're giving me their usual divided attention, tapping their fingers, looking at their watches, clearing their throats, contemplating the ceiling or otherwise revealing that they're simply not all there.

On the other hand, I remember one man in my life who was *real there*. When you talked with Luther Wesley Smith (a clergyman—how could he have been anything else!—he was a denominational publishing and educational genius) you got the impression that you were the only person in the world who mattered at that moment; his was a complete be-in. One of the busiest men in my life, he was one of the most alive men I have ever known.

Thereness is the ability to give yourself fully. Though the verse in Ecclesiastes, "Whatsoever thy hand findeth to do, do it with thy might," has been used to cover a multitude of sins, it's a good text for a be-in that presupposes some guiding mind, some selectivity of faith. If you're going to do it, do it! If you're going to listen, listen! If you're going to speak, speak! If you're going to live, live!

There is no more humiliating repudiation of faith, of the love of God, of the brotherhood of Christ, of the companioning of the Holy Spirit, than to worry your way through life; than to be afraid to enjoy, enjoy; than to hold back from ever committing yourself utterly to something or someone; than constantly to seek for a place to hide from new ideas. Was it Dwight L. Moody who said that saving faith is not just sitting down in the chair, but propping your feet up, tilting back, committing your whole weight to it? Well, life itself is like that. And one of the big tragedies of life is the number of Christians who are scared to death to sit down, to trust their weight to anything.

God surely doesn't intend for us to be spiritual schizophrenics, our minds half in our world and half in his. It's one world, and it's all his.

Our pious tricks don't make any difference to God, any more than the subterfuge of the little woman flying for the first time made any difference, but they make considerable difference to our own well-being: "I didn't put my full weight down on the seat," she said.

For better or worse, we're aboard planet earth, and it seems to me more faithful than faithless, more sacred than secular, for the

Christian to enjoy the ride. Indeed, who should enjoy it more?

There are probably a couple of reasons why we hesitate to live a particular experience to the full. One is our inherited suspicion of pleasures, and if we call them pleasures "of the flesh," they sound even worse. I have nothing against pleasures of the spirit, for they are considerable. But "the flesh" is where we happen to be, and though it sounds faintly sacrilegious to say it, this is where Jesus was, too. To deny the reality of our physical attributes and capabilities is to make of our bodies something less than the temples they are. Can we not be *fully* men without being less than men?

Then there is another reason, and that is our fear of being hurt. Boughs break. Therefore, do not commit yourself to the bough. You lose the one you love by death or in some other manner. Therefore, do not commit yourself to love. You play the Good Samaritan and the police want to know all about what happened and why you took that trouble if *you* weren't guilty, and it becomes exceedingly bothersome. Therefore, don't get involved.

The thing is that hurt is of itself part of the wholeness of living. Furthermore, the risk of it is part of the wholeness of faith. Take out the getting hurt and you would take out everything significant about Christianity, including the cross. Put to one side all those who have been hurt because they lived out their humanness in their caring, and the place you put them you could call heaven. Those who are afraid to live are already partly dead. Those who are (and who have been) wholly alive will never be fully dead.

Perhaps that was what Jesus meant when he said, "For whosoever will save his life shall lose it; but whosoever shall lose his life for my sake . . . the same shall save it."

It's a great life! For Christ's sake, live it up!

But it is your life. When you do your living, you'll have to do it your own way, for you are you.

7) How do I look,
everybody?

One gets the feeling that there are a lot of people who are more interested in how they look doing a job than they are in getting the job done. The notion that pose makes the man is in evidence in all sorts of endeavors where wheels are spinning madly but nothing important is happening. If you want to make a big thing of running a powerboat, for example, this notion says that while it's helpful to know something about navigation, weather, where you're going and the like, it's absolutely necessary to have an admiral's cap.

I remember my own cultural shock when, after being brought up believing that all railroad engineers wore bulky, blue-and-white-striped caps, I moved to New York and found that engineers on my commuter train usually didn't wear any kind of head covering, and when they did, it was as likely as not to be an old fedora. There was something very un-engineering, even un-railroading, about it, to me. That the fellow with the fedora could get trains from one place to another with total competence seemed to me to be almost beside the point.

How much money people spend to look like whatever it is they want to be, I have no idea, but I imagine it is considerable. The way to look like a woodworker is to buy a basement-full of power tools. The way to look like a tycoon is to rent an office with ceiling-to-floor windows, wall-to-wall carpeting, and a wrap-around desk. Nobody's supposed to ask what once were reasonable questions, like, "What have you built?" or "How much business are you doing?" We've progressed from wondering how a man can drive a train if he doesn't wear an engineer's cap to assuming that anybody can drive a train if he puts an engineer's cap on his head.

It has to do with "image," which is a big word these days with presidents, corporations, and everybody with something to sell— which includes just about all of us. Our first thought is not as often, "*Are* we good?" as it is, "Do we *look* good?" Some presidents have even worried, so it is said, about what history would say of them—anxiety in perpetuity. Some Christians feel the same way about the Day of Judgment. When you get concerned about whether you're looking like a president or a preacher or a parent or a Christian or a tycoon, there's the strong chance that to this extent you are neglecting the job of presiding or preaching or living or tycooning or whatever.

Imagine, for example, Thomas Edison sitting down and saying, "Now what does today's high-powered inventor look like?" and letting his eyebrows grow bushy because he figured that is what inventors did and curling up for a nap on his rolltop desk because he figured that is the way they slept. He invented because he had a restless, questing mind, not because he had a Faraday coil and an electrolytic cell.

Jesus, as far as I can tell, never asked himself, "Is this the way a Messiah would do it?" Paul never said, "If I'm going to look like a great missionary, maybe I ought to take off for Ephesus." Noah never said, "Speaking as an eminent shipbuilder. . . ." They were wrapped up in what they were doing, not in how they looked. When you get right down to it, none of them looked very good. If Jesus had had a public relations manager, he would have cautioned, "Whatever you do, don't be seen with sinners—it will ruin your image." In fact, Peter, who tried his best to run a tidy shop, public relations-wise, counseled in effect, "Don't go to Jerusalem!" and Jesus retorted with the line we now use in jest but which was devastating then, "Get thee behind me, Satan."

Jesus simply didn't care how he looked. If he had, he wouldn't have healed on the Sabbath or made men angry at being forced to examine their own poses. He wouldn't have told the story about the man who had posed so long that he didn't know a phony when he was being one—the man who went up to the Temple to pray in a spot where the light showed off his pious profile to best advantage.

We have got this matter of how we look all mixed up, in and out of church, with how we believe. For one thing, there's that verse, "Abstain from all appearance of evil" (I Thess. 5:22, K.J.V.), which has been used to protect more poses than you can shake a stick at. The assumed advice is that the farther you can stay away from anybody who is an undesirable character, the better. Don't be seen talking at the well with a prostitute. Don't take the once-crooked tax collector into your circle of friends. It's bad for your image.

That verse troubled me, too, until I happened to look it up in the Revised Standard Version. There it reads, "Abstain from every form of evil." And that's different! To abstain from all *appearance* of evil, one would have to be like those three little monkeys, with eyes, ears, and mouth covered—and some Christians have incorporated exactly that timid trinity into their theology. And yet, how terrribly much faith needs to see! How terribly much faith needs to hear! How terribly much faith needs to be involved! And appearances be hanged!

There is a reverse twist on this that also makes us less than we ought to be. Our obsession with the looks of things pushes us into self-conscious justifications for doing what we ought to be doing without apology. Stop to give aid to some unconventionally unfortunate person, and forever after, as you tell the story, you feel compelled to explain, "I was just passing by, and—." You have to make clear that these were not your usual haunts and that you did not ordinarily associate with publicans and sinners of this type. You were just passing by and what else could you do? Well, that's better than passing by on the other side, but not much better.

The Samaritan, when he saw a man in trouble, didn't stop to consider whether he wanted to be the Good Samaritan or the Bad Samaritan or what the innkeeper would think when he hauled the victim in on his donkey and asked for a room. Maybe the innkeeper suspected *him* of being involved. Maybe the innkeeper wondered why a man of means was getting mixed up in a mess like this. But no apologies, no justifications. A man needed help. That was the adequate explanation.

I remember a couple of shabby explanations of my own in my younger days, and I am ashamed of them. I did something I thought was quite magnanimous, and prefaced it with the statement, "Because I'm a Christian. . . ." Another time, when I made a decision not to oppose the sale of property to a Negro, I said, "Because I am a minister. . . ." What I should have said in both cases was, "Because I am a *human being*. . ."!

I can't imagine Jesus going about doing good, explaining, "Because I am the Son of God. . . ." When John the Baptist sent emissionaries to him to ask, "Are you he?" Jesus didn't say, "Yes." He said, "Go and tell John the blind receive their sight and the lame walk, lepers are cleansed and the deaf hear." Goodness, rightness, is inherent, of the essence. It does not require one to cringe behind a principle or rule or costume or chapter and verse.

How important, anyway, are the "appearances" we think we have to keep up? Why don't we try, for a change, to be simply what we are—and get on with it?

This may mean "doing your own thing." Or sometimes it may mean something quite different.

8) When you can't do your own thing— what then?

Then you do someone else's thing. Next question.

This bit about "doing your own thing" started out as a good idea, a needed point of view, a neglected piece of wisdom. But somewhere along the line it became overemphasized, which is to say it was distorted—a fate which can happen to the best of directives and doctrines. And it happened in the same way that it happens to them: What was *a* truth came to be regarded as *the* truth. Instead of being taken for the push to selfhood that in reality it is, it was debased by being elevated into an apology which was presumed to cover every form of action imaginable. Anything went, if you just flipped back your lapel and disclosed the rationale, "I'm only doing my thing!"

In our kind of world—and as far as I can tell, it has been the same kind of world since anyone can remember or books have been written—the chances are that you and I will be doing someone else's thing oftener than we will be doing our own. The someone else may be a wife or husband. It may be a son or daughter. It may be a mother or father. It may be the Boy Scouts or the YWCA. It may be the pastor, the president of the women's guild, or the church nominating committee. It may be a teacher. It may be neighbors next door or an earth's diameter away. It may be a generation yet unborn. It may be an employer or, for that matter, an employee. It may be a coworker. It may be the fellow who sets up the train or plane or postal pickup schedules. It may be the credit bureau. It may be the policeman on the corner or a legislator in Washington. By the very act of living, breathing, believing, we mortgage one parcel after another of our independence. The only part that changes with the passing of people and time is the mortgagee.

And yet, the obligation to do someone else's thing is not the whole truth, either, and it was reaction against *that* which set off the own-thing emphasis. The difficulty with keeping a balance between self and others is the difficulty, as someone has pointed out, of looking at a pyramid: you can, at best, see from the surrounding desert only half of it at a time. Take the someone-else perspective 100 per cent and you have no opportunity to be literally yourself. You're at the mercy of others. You jump when they call, and not until they do. You are thereby relieved, you may think, of all responsibility for your actions, for you are not your own man or woman—an expression that, interestingly enough, is often heard in politics disparagingly and in religion approvingly. And yet, who would wish to say of Jesus that he was not his own man? He *was*—excitingly, utterly!

Doing someone else's thing may be the ultimate in Christian faith or the ultimate in faithlessness. It may be the grand commitment or the Christian cop-out. This could depend upon which someone else is giving the orders you're taking, and what, under the circumstances, is your own thing. In wartime Germany, for example, someone else's thing was decidedly unacceptable in retrospect, if the someone was Hitler. But Hitler Germany is fast becoming ancient history. The citizen of America also has to reconcile somehow his personal integrity and his social integrity.

It would be nice if there were a neat, clean formula for the proper combination—so large a percentage for self, so large for others. But there is no formula, and besides, the percentages may be different at different times—which neither the rigid rulebook Christian nor the equally rigid situational-ethics Christian seems to be able to admit. The Good Samaritan presumably had earned the money he paid to the innkeeper on behalf of the man who fell among thieves. When was *he* doing "his own thing"? When he was earning his keep or when he was paying somebody else's? Was he "good" only when he was giving, or was he as good a Samaritan on his job as he was on the road? In other words, was his goodness—his thing—something he put on now and then or was it his style of life, inseparable from the man himself?

The way all this is coming out, it seems to me, is that your own thing and somebody else's thing cannot be sold separately, either from the pulpit or from Haight-Ashbury. They are in this respect like table salt, which, chemically speaking, is a combination of sodium and chlorine. Separate salt into its components, and you've got something, but it isn't salt. Whatever it is, you had better not sprinkle it on the meat. Maybe that's why, scripturally, "we" are so seldom the "ye" who can honestly be called the salt of the earth—we have decided we're going to be this *or* that, when what it takes is to be this *and* that.

We simply cannot escape the relationships—and responsibilities— of living together in the same country and the same world. We have mislabeled what we practice in America as the free-enterprise system, when no enterprise system is or can be free. It is an interacting enterprise system. But with all the historic talk of free enterprise in business, why then does it seem so strange that there should have come a drumming up of other kinds of "free enterprise"—love, religion, art, literature? What we neglected to impart was that nothing is free. There is a discipline that makes a poem a poem, that makes love love, that makes faith faith, that makes people a functioning society. Sure, you can do your own thing! But who wants to live in a country where two hundred million people are doing their own thing, or ride on an airline where everybody is doing his own thing, or even worship in a church where three hundred people are doing it?

Where does the Christian fit into all this? How does he keep from going off one deep end or another? One thing he does, it seems to me, is to accept the possibility that up to a point, doing someone else's thing may *be* his thing. Not blindly. Not by thinking less but by thinking more. Not by living less but by living more. Not by being less the man but more the man. Not by being less concerned, but more concerned. Not by protectiveness, even where faith is concerned, but by living confidently—out on the thin edge of faith, very often. Which is quite different from living out on the thin edge of selfishness. For the Christian, the someone else whose thing he does may very well be Someone Else.

As a Christian, I have no mandate to put less of my own thing—which is to say, my own self—into what I do. My mandate is to put more of it in. Indeed, it is to put all of it in.

9) Wholly, Wholly, Wholly

I was attending a Sunday morning worship service in a brand-new church building. An airy, pleasant sanctuary it was, smelling of varnish, laminated wood, and carpeting. As the service progressed and I had opportunity to study the furnishings, my eye was drawn toward the lighting fixtures, hanging from the ceiling. Cylinders of frosted off-white glass, they were set in metal frames that divided the glass into three vertical sections. On each of these sections, I noticed that a metal cross perhaps six inches high was affixed to the glass, three crosses to each light. The designer's intent, I assumed, was that one of the crosses could thus be seen from any angle, rather than that the three were symbolic of the Trinity or that they stood for the three crosses on Calvary, in which case two of them would have belonged to thieves.

I imagined the thought processes that went into the designing of those lights: "This is to be a religious lighting fixture, right? Then we put crosses on it, right?"

The implication is that putting a cross on a light makes it a Christian light and that the beauty of the lighting fixture itself doesn't do it, the amount of light it gives doesn't do it, the manner in which the fixture harmonizes with the architecture doesn't do it, the quality of the craftsmanship doesn't do it, the excellence of the materials doesn't do it.

Though all inadvertently, this raises certain questions: (1) Would putting a Christian label on a bad light make it a good light? (2) Would what is in reality a good light be a bad light without the label?

To put it another way, so that we can begin to think about people instead of lights—Is Christianity of the essence, or is it something you paste on at the end of the production line? Is the Christian so indistinguishable in life-style, in zest, in love, in compassion, in the general confident excitement of living, that he must be labeled, "This is a Christian," the way a child's drawing must be labeled, "This is a cat"?

Now, when it comes to lighting fixtures, it's not a big matter, except that conceivably a cross might be used to dignify shoddiness. For who could then say, "That light doesn't look religious to me"? I must admit that when I sometimes have heard it said that art has to have integrity, I thought it was another example of obscure art-critic-type talk. But I think I see now what they were driving at. Things must be and do, as well as it is possible to be and do, whatever they are supposed to be and do. This means that using (dwell for a moment on that word *using*) easy, quickie gimmicks or labels or symbols to identify qualities that are not of themselves apparent— even and especially if that label happens to be the cross—is to lessen and demean one's credibility as artist, person, or Christian. It is essence, integrity, reality that evokes deep-calling-to-deep response. Art must be first art for art's sake before it can be art for something or someone else's sake.

There have been times for me when I would not have recognized some Christians if they had not been carefully labeled. Even then I wasn't sure. And I must confess that there have been times when I would not have been recognizable without a label. This places a heavy burden upon labels—a burden they simply cannot bear. For what eventually happens—and it doesn't take very long—is that instead of the label squeaking us through, we diminish the label.

We have paid more attention to the label than to the product on which the label appears. We've somehow got in the habit-forming frame of mind that faith, commitment, witness is an additive, a pious put-on. It just hasn't hit us that there has to be something intrinsic, something of the essence, something at the center of personality and life which marks the Christian—marks him more subtly, perhaps, than a label, but more indelibly, too.

The "in" labels that we make sure can be seen when we drape our faith over the back of the pew vary from time to time, from church to church, from group to group. Bible-carrying and Bible-quoting are a required label in some of them. There is certainly nothing wrong with either practice, so long as it is more than a password. "Thy word have I hid in my heart," was David's put-in alternative to a scriptural put-on. Some Christians are hiding it on a bookshelf; compulsively possessing an unread Bible is, of course, its own kind of put-on.

There are particular words which are labels, ranging from "blood" in one church to "relevance" in another. There are words I go to any length to avoid, not because they are meaningless but because I refuse to be coerced into giving passwords in order to gain admittance to something. I would rather stay in God's outdoors, where the best response one can make sometimes is a heart-brimming and soul shaking silence, an inarticulate groan of spirit, a humbling bafflement of mind, even a shattering but strangely liberating doubt. There is so little one can say in a password; to use one always requires paring down one's own spirit so that it may fit precisely against some other's. To demand one means that the demander cares only secondarily about what a person is, primarily about what he says.

Time and again, Jesus deflated seeming as against being. When rules of one sort or another got in the way of what the rules were supposed to promote, he ignored them. He healed on the Sabbath, so logically and utterly defying a pious no-no that the precedent he established now reveals any other course to be not only inhuman but ungodly. On another Sabbath his disciples picked a few heads of grain as they walked with him through a field, rolled them in their hands to separate kernels from chaff, and popped the kernels into their mouths. Religious nit-pickers accused them of "threshing," a gnat that had to be magnified before it could be strained out, while wholesale camel-swallowings went on daily in town and temple with no slightest discomfort to the legalists. Jesus simply would not mouth their puny passwords. His first concern was not the rule that the man was to obey, but the man who was to obey the rule. If that sounds faintly subversive, keep in mind that Jesus said it first: "The Sabbath was made for man, not man for the Sabbath."

When an adulteress caught in the act was brought to him for judgment (his as well as hers), her accusers saw a broken law. He saw a broken woman.

When he went to dinner with the wrong people, the self-righteous rulebook-quoting, password-demanding, label-reading religious leaders saw winebibbers and sinners. Jesus knew what his hosts were, but evidently he preferred generous honest sinners who enjoyed living life to penny-pinching hypocritical sinners who did not. Besides, there is no evidence in the record that those who criticized the tablemates of Jesus ever themselves invited him home to dinner or even to lunch.

You would think that after getting through the New Testament in retrospect, the rest of us would have learned some things we appear not to have learned!

One of our unlearned lessons concerns stewardship. We're still quibbling about bits and pieces. The password here has been the word "tithe," which means one-tenth. Stewardship has been tied up for some Christians in a neat little bundle called the tenth. And while debate rages on this pinhead about figuring it on gross or net, or whether it should go into the "storehouse" or shouldn't, we completely ignore the fact that stewardship concerns not one-tenth but ten-tenths. Where does it say, "He who loses one-tenth of his life for my sake will find it"? Stewardship is not a classroom exercise in fractions. It is a homework assignment in total living.

There is an inescapable totality about life and faith. In a staggering sense, it's all or nothing. The demand is for a life-style, a point of view, an outlook, an inlook, an uplook that is so distinguishably Christian that it doesn't have to depend upon a label for its impact.

Lord, that I may be *whole*!

10) Secularism is nice, when it comes in a paycheck

Wholeness requires living in two worlds at the same time—the world of why and the world of what—and it's a neat trick to keep your balance. One world or the other—and they're usually called flesh and spirit, or body and soul—is always being downgraded by somebody. The usual target of pulpit wrath is body, flesh, the measurable world of the seeable and touchable and spendable. The pulpit name for it is secularism.

Secularism certainly *sounds* like something that should be contended against, to the last earnest drop of secular blood. But on second thought, all you have to do to make even a fairly innocent word quite subversive looking is to put *ism* on the end of it. Perhaps the way to really measure a word is to take the *ism* away and see how it looks by itself. Do that with secularism and you wind up with "secular," which doesn't sound half so bad. For that matter, it appears to be quite decent and maybe even important.

Yet, when you put "secular" against another word with which it is often contrasted—"sacred"—it gets second billing every time. Either that, or it gets the "two-hand" treatment—sacred on the one hand, and secular on the other hand. As is usually the case with two hands, one doesn't know what the other is doing and in this case, one doesn't seem much to care.

There is some caring in one respect: some of the very preachers who are denouncing secularism the loudest are doing their best to infiltrate it, convert it. They are saying, "Be Christian on Monday as well as on Sunday. Be Christian on the job as well as in church. Be Christian in the pocketbook department as well as in the prayer department. Let works square with faith, deed with creed." And nobody can argue about that, though I have the sneaking suspicion that faith will always be a *little* out in front of works, else what's an incentive for? The antisecularists are as enamored of secularism as the next man, if only by their desire to have it work for them and theirs. When it does, that puts a halo around it.

Let a prominent businessman, for example, or a movie star, or a political leader join a church or become affiliated with some religious project or other, and the drums begin beating and the mimeographs grinding. He or she is televised, paraded, pointed to, photographed— as if to say, "See, the impossible has happened! Here is a *Christian* businessman, movie star, actor, Senator! If it can happen to a person like this, it can happen to anyone!" And yet, one does not get the impression that any particular honor is being paid to the vocation, but rather that the vocation is being used—exploited even—and that probably the publicist would be a lot happier if whoever it was got out of whatever the secular job, however glamorous, happened to be and got into something "sacred."

That's one side of the story. But at the same time that secularism has become the enemy of God and the current scapegoat for almost everything that ails us, we are being reminded by some other theologians, amateur and professional, that the distinctions between the sacred and the secular are artificial, misleading, disturbing, and altogether phony. To say that *this* is sacred while *that* is not or is less so, is, they hold, indefensible. Many of the ills of life, they say, have been caused by this unfortunate wall of separation that makes one place holier than another; one day holier than another; certain words, men, women, and manners of dress holier than others.

It's not, they hold, a matter of being Christian on Monday as well as Sunday—what *better* time to be Christian? It's not a matter of being Christian on the job as well as in church—how, actually, do you go about being Christian in church? It's not a matter of counting out the dollars, "one for You, nine for me," but of regarding every dollar, however spent, as a divine trust with stewardship involving ten out of ten.

This leads me to observe that as far as faith and works are concerned, James came up with an interesting headline long before God was declared to be dead, and one even more revolutionary: "Faith is dead," said James "unless validated on the job." It seems to me that if faith without works is dead, so is faith without workmen. And if not everyone can be a professional Christian, there are going to have to be a lot of amateur Christians who are at the same time professional farmers and bricklayers. To paraphrase Paul: "If the businessman shall say, because I am not a director of Christian education, my job is a profane one; is his job really profane? . . . If the whole community were the preacher, who would do the plumbing?"

In the same vein we speak of a "religious novel" or a "religious motion picture," as if either has to be about a particular topic in order to be religious. For jobs, we have of course developed a whole scale of holiness. Preachers, bishops, and such are presumed to be somewhere at or near the top of the list. It shades off into the "secular" with physicians rated as almost sacred, for they treat the bodies that God created, and farmers, for they till the soil that God created. But the garbage collector, who has a certain relationship to those same products the farmer produces, comes out looking fairly secular. All of which is nonsense.

As is true of novels and films, so I would guess it is true of vocations, that sacredness is not so much something we find in them as it is something we bring to them. There is that side of it—but also there is a certain inherent holiness, a certain wholeness, a certain integrity in the craft which may or may not be recognized by the craftsman, but which contributes to order and community in God's world. I probably will not ask the plumber, when I call him, if he is a Christian. I will ask him if he can repair the leaking pipe. If he cannot fix the pipe, his religious commitment, though admirable and even deep, will not do it either. His faith may be of aid to me in other ways—and about then I may need all I can get—but it will not fix my pipe. I would rather he be both a Christian and a plumber, for then we will have fellowship on two levels, but at that moment it is— dare I say it?—more important to me that he be a plumber, and I will thank God for his plumbing skill. His secularism can be terribly sacred to me right then.

As for the Christian, his job—whatever it is—*must* be Christian, for that is where he is, that is what he does. That is his channel and therefore it becomes God's channel. And if it is God's also, it is not profane, not secular, but a holy place, and possibly even the holy of holies. Work is not something you get out of the way so that you can begin to live, begin to be holy, begin to seek the sacred. It is where God is as much as he is anywhere else. Every dollar earned is a sacred dollar, for it is a little piece of human life.

At the same time, the collection plate on a Sunday morning is the essence of secularism. Every coin and bill there was generated by commerce, and nobody seems to be objecting very strongly. The dollars that pay the church mortgage, that support missionaries, that pay the pastors and evangelists (even those who are unhappy about secularism) are secular dollars, generated by "secular" pursuit. Nobody, so far as I know, turns them down on that account.

Of course, there is a danger in upgrading our jobs from secular to sacred rating. If everybody is holy, may it be that nothing would seem holy? Would Christmas every day of the year be Christmas *any* day of the year? If we lived as if God were in everything, would it seem as if God were nowhere? Do we require a holier-than? Perhaps. But say to yourself, "Mine is a sacred vocation. Mine is a holy calling." And then watch it become just that.

11) O Beautiful for Crowded Cities

When I visualize the ideal church, it always comes out looking like the little white spire-topped meetinghouse on a hilltop in eastern Ohio, where my father attended services as boy and youth. My paternal grandmother and grandfather, neither of whom I ever knew, lie under the green turf behind the church, and names on the church-yard stones are ones I heard mentioned often. I have been to the little church only five times or so during the years, usually at home-comings. Remembering the church, standing on its hilltop and visible when I was yet far distant, quickens my pulse even now.

The last time I was back, the growing village was creeping toward the modest white frame building. The road in front had become a highway, and the secondary road that cuts off at the side of the church-yard to drop down the west side of the hill already had whittled away at the church property. Sooner or later houses and perhaps apartment buildings will move closer and closer and the roads will grow wider and wider. The remote hilltop will no longer be remote and the spire no longer will be a beckoning finger for all who travel up the valley from Irondale and Yellow Creek. The possibility that by then a more adequate building may replace it does not altogether ease my disquiet, nor the fact that if there is anything a church needs it is people—to serve and to be served—and that if the little church survives it will someday be up to its eaves in people.

My trouble, you see, is the same ailment that afflicts and has afflicted American Christendom very nearly to the death: so many of us have been and still are little-brown-church-in-the-wildwood or little-white-church-on-the-hill people. But there is a dearth of wildwood these days, and as any demographic study indicates, we haven't seen anything, wildwoodwise, yet. The dear, dead days! Lot's wife today is immobilized by her longing look at the countryside, not the city, and she has whole congregations of companionship—pillars of salt that have lost their savor. I don't want to be in that number, when the saints stand looking back.

How did we get this way? The Cowper Syndrome had something to do with it. In his poem, "The Task," William Cowper wrote, "God made the country, and man made the town," and people fell for it. Much if not practically all of the rest of the poem (it runs to six books with hundreds of lines in each) has been overlooked, but with his town-and-country pronouncement, he achieved epigrammatic immortality. Indicative of the lack of perspicacity in his famous line is his vain hope in Book II:

> *Oh for a lodge in some vast wilderness,*
> *Some boundless contiguity of shade,*
> *Where rumour of oppression and deceit,*
> *Of unsuccessful or successful war,*
> *Might never reach me more.*

You can hardly join that kind of lodge any more—though we must keep in mind he was writing in 1785, a good year for wildwood.

In Book IV he remarks:

> *'Tis pleasant, through the loopholes of retreat,*
> *To peep at such a world, to see the stir*
> *Of the great Babel; and not feel the crowd.*

One can only say of that, " 'Tis, indeed." Or more to the point, " 'Twould be." For, alas, it can't be done. To feel the stir, you have to be in the crowd, jostled by it, receive its elbows in your ribs. The trouble with bucolic Christendom to date is that it has evidently produced a bigger supply of peeping Thomases than Babel-rousers. The adventurous uncommitted yearn to be where the action is, and the action most often is not where the safely committed are most likely to be found. The action has to be where people are, and it stands to reason that the more people, the greater the action and interaction. Whatever the Fall of Man means doctrinally, it does not give anyone or any church license to take to the hills on the Thurberish theological grounds that "people are no damn good" and that the fewer of them in a given square mile, the better for the saints.

Cowper isn't the only one guilty of the spiritual downgrading of cities. Many of our hymns are rural-oriented, not to mention "America, the Beautiful." Spacious skies, amber waves of grain, purple mountains, and fruited plain get top billing. Alabaster cities receive a passing mention in the final stanza, but, "undimmed by human tears," these cities are only prophetic ones, unrealized and perhaps unrealizable. There is, I submit, a beauty and a glory in the city as it is, tears and all.

The city is where more and more of us are living, and if we are not living there, we are working there. It is the city that is the economic heart of the nation. Though there is more to country than farms, one measure of what is happening is the dropping farm population—down by three million in four years. When the U.S. Census Bureau lumped into "rural" everything possible, the total was only 54 million against an urban population of 125 million. And that was the 1960 figure. Like it or not, we're more and more huddling together for warmth. If we have to find, or reveal, God in the wide open spaces, then God is simply not going to be available to most of us. As one inner-city pastor put it, "If only in the rustling grass we hear Him pass, He's not going to be heard." And if the church is tied to a rustling-grass concept of Christianity, the concrete and asphalt crowd will have to look elsewhere for relevance. They are doing just that.

The metropolis in turn is being swallowed by the megalopolis. You hear such expressions as "Greater Los Angeles" or "Chicagoland," meaning that except for the Rotary Club signs, the visitor can't tell when he's out of the city proper and into a satellite community. The Atlantic seaboard from Boston to Washington, D.C., they tell us, is one big urban sprawl. There's no place for that urban population line on the graph to go but up.

Meanwhile, back at the church, the rural vote is weighted, just as it has been in so many state legislatures, and when you think of heaven, you probably think of rolling fields and Holstein cows. I'm a Holstein man myself, but for the average American to whom the church had better be finding something to say, milk comes in cardboard cartons, not in cows. We've been building little brown churches in the cities and operating them with little brown church ideas and with little brown church theology. We've in effect made museums of churches, memorializing in them something that once was and is no more. On that, we've surpassed even the Russians; at least they turned out the congregations before they made *their* churches into museums.

I confess that I love rural America and that I enjoy wide spaces, when I can find them. I personally resent the encroaching shopping centers and the mounting school taxes. I'd rather look at a grove of trees than at a rooftop any day of the week, including Sunday. But it's rapidly becoming a luxury for me. And it has been for years a luxury for the churches. At the same time, I know that country life is not necessarily more devout than city life. The Uniform Crime Reports issued by the F.B.I. show that.

As for the ravaging of the outdoors, the city has no monopoly on this. Among the most distressing slums I have ever seen, the most ramshackle dwellings, littered yards, God-forsaken hopelessness, have been those in the country.

The cities have their slums, but the cities also have their own beauty. The other morning when I was coming to work, New York City sparkled in the clean morning sunlight. I inhaled as deeply as

I dared, looked up at the tall buildings—they, too, are God's creations—and was glad to be alive. I felt like bursting into "The Holy City," substituting the name of mine for Jerusalem!

Here in the city is where most of us are, and here is where the church must be, in spirit as well as spire. And for all the backward-lookers, Cowper does have this one grain of encouragement: "Who loves a garden loves a greenhouse too."

12) So you're feeling great?
Great!

In city or in country, there's something about feeling good that we mistrust. Those comparatively few times when we're tempted to throw wide the arms in joyous abandon, take a deep, delighted breath, and shout, "I'm glad to be alive!" something in our heritage and conscience tries to scowl us down.

Not only are our spiritual genes crammed with the strait-laced, sober-sided, no-nonsense life-style of our Puritan ancestors, but we're getting a new dose from contemporary unscarred liberals. Christianity is becoming more than ever a defensive, unsmiling, unhappy way of life, and that's a pity.

I think there must have been a few bouncy Puritans, and I know for sure there are some radiant Christians today. Radiance, victorious living, aliveness, glow, whatever you want to call it, is achieved to the degree to which one dares to relate in utter honesty to God and all God's children. Radiance is not canceled out by concern. The two are, in fact, inseparable. The phony among us, and in us, whether Puritan or liberal, is he who is not dirtying his hands with Christian compassion (and compassion is never sterile or antiseptic), but who is trying to look as if he is. This gives him the reverse of "the appearance of evil" and is what he assumes to be the appearance of concern. But it has none of the joyous excitement of committed faith.

Paul concluded a sentence to the Ephesians with the words, ". . . having done all, to stand," not, ". . . having done nothing, to stand," which latter is the customary clean-hands-bleeding-heart approach. I mean, if lamenting is *all* you have in mind, then you had jolly well better throw yourself into it. If, on the other hand, you *do* something, and don't just look as if you might do it any minute, there is not quite so much left to lament about. The word that takes at least some pouches from under the eyes of the psyche is "involvement." The involved person is less likely, it seems to me, to be a pessimist than is the uninvolved person whose only contribution to the general welfare is impotent handwringing or arrogant isolation.

Our fear and guilt in the presence of joy have two roots, neither of which is Christian. First, it is almost as if we suspect God of the unkindest cut of all—being nice to us before he lets the roof fall in. Sheer exultation is, under those circumstances, not appropriate, for things are bound to get worse. Second, feeling good when all about are feeling bad looks in these parlous times like social treason, which apparently is the worst of the few theological heresies that continue to have any impact today.

Even those who do not restrain their optimism for presumed religious reasons still choose to play it with as few risks as possible. Is there something left over from an era when faith was dim and Druidic in such an abruptly stifled cheer as, "I haven't had a flat tire all summer—*knock on wood*"? Christians may not actually knock on wood, but those most likely not to may be the selfsame people who have a knock-on-wood clause written into their theology. For that is simply another way of accommodating to a theology of despair, which, as you may have noticed, is much in circulation these days and which some of its practitioners, I do believe, find dolefully and immensely enjoyable.

There is certainly much in the world that is terribly, terribly wrong and cause for grief. One scarcely knows where to start the catalog of horror. Racism would have to be somewhere near the top of the list, for it is a root of many evils, including many if not most of our wars. That it is still possible to discriminate thinkingly—or worse, unthinkingly—against any human being because of skin color defies logic and reason as well as faith. Whites (and some blacks) have a vested interest in prejudice and show few signs of doing anything about it, an utterly depressing fact of life. But turning a wall into a wailing wall doesn't make it less a wall and may actually make it more a wall.

And the wars go on. If the American people did not think they were getting their worth in money and blood in Indochina, they would have stopped the war—another depressing thought. There is always a general who is ready to retake a Hamburger Hill, even if it "costs him" a division. A division is at least five thousand men, and it wouldn't cost him nearly as much as it would cost five thousand mothers and fathers and wives (to say nothing of their sons and husbands). War is indeed hell, and we cannot pray it pure.

Children are hungry, and the by-product sadness is that nowadays even to say no more than that is to be accused of making a political statement. The same charge comes quickly if one should say that refugees in Jordan after twenty years deserve something better than tents. Or that refugees in Israel deserve security, too. We seem to be on dead center (the expression is peculiarly apt) with respect to so many of the world's problems, and this is grief in itself.

In our own land, there is shocking hunger, ill-housing, all kinds of deprivation. Not only are these to be found assuredly in our land but likely in our town and perhaps on our street, especially if it's one of those long streets that changes character and sometimes name as it goes its way.

Even leaving out man's inhumanity to man, there is still "humanity's" inhumanity to man to wipe off an unwary grin and cut one down to size. There are the "natural" tragedies, the accidents of birth and life and death, illness, the fears of coming into the world and going out of it, the sadnesses of partings of assorted kinds and durations.

How in the world—how in this kind of world—is it possible to feel "good"? Isn't joy the supreme blasphemy in a world like ours?

It might be if it *were* our world, but it isn't. We manage to put considerable zest into a Sunday singing of "This Is My Father's World." If it's his world on Sunday, it's his on Saturday night. In sickness and in health, it's his. And if it's his, how can we *not* take heart, just at being in it?

To put it another way, where in the face of our crazy, messed-up, mixed-up existence is there any room for the luxury of despair? Not joy but hopelessness is the supreme blasphemy. Personally, I think that long-facedness has done and is doing more harm than two-facedness, though you will normally find only the latter on the standard, certified church sin list.

Would you believe that heavy-heartedness is something that some people *pray* for? The customary word is "burden," as in "Lord, give me a burden for souls . . . or for missions . . . or for this or that." Burden, if it means anything, means weight. The request is to feel weight, to feel guilt for not feeling guilty. Yet, presumably even this request is qualified, for such seekers do not precisely define how constant a burden they are seeking, how continuous a guilt pressure they are asking for, or what they will settle for. Should it be all the time, half of the time, one-eighth of the time, one-tenth—a tithe— of the time? And do they expect to be at their winsome best in their most burdened moments?

I don't know how it is with you, but I've seen too many people who too obviously had the burden and nothing else, to be attracted by them. Religious radiance does more for me. Personally, I dread turning into a sour picky-picky person for whom all the life has gone out of faith. I dread ever being so crushed by the weight of earth or heaven (or hell, for that matter), that I can't take that deep breath and say from the toes up, "Isn't it *great* just to be alive!" This despite the condition of things in general and of me in particular. This despite what may come tomorrow and what will inevitably come, sooner or later.

Now, this minute, I'm alive and this is God's world.

Talk about praying! There's a prayer for you. It gives God at least some credit for knowing what he's doing. It affirms. It celebrates.

It doesn't make me less caring about sorrow, my own and that of others, but makes me more able to cope with it. It brings me *up* to my full stature.

For the kind of living we are called upon to do today, we need all the stature we can get. And if today is where the joy is, it's also where the job is.

13) In the
meantime

More problems could be solved by a meantime-theology than this world dreams of. Nothing is more with us than meantime. Yet it generally gets not much more than an afterthought. When we're finished making our grand plans for the future, we quit talking, as if there is nothing else to talk about or we throw in as a last-minute concession, "But in the meantime. . . ."

Yet, the meantime is where life is lived, where decisions are made, where pain is suffered, where we are lonely and glad, where we laugh and cry. There is the joy of anticipation. But in the meantime . . .? There is the life beyond, whatever and wherever it turns out to be. But in the meantime . . .? We hope for domestic tranquillity, liberty, and justice for all. But in the meantime . . .? There will finally be peace in Southeast Asia. But in the meantime . . .? There will some-day have to be a more equitable distribution of this nation's and this world's goods. But in the meantime . . .? Simple arithmetic says something about the future of racial relationships in South Africa and Rhodesia. But in the meantime . . .? Tomorrow I will begin dieting or quit smoking or make up my mind about this or that. But in the meantime . . .?

Why should not the meantime reflect what we know is surely going

to happen or what we believe should happen? Why must the meantime so consistently obstruct the inevitable or the desirable?

We act so often as if there is all the future in the world and no
meantime. Actually, we've got more meantime than most of us have
the courage to use. We just let it sit there.

It's easier, for example, to project our unfinished business upon
God than to get on with it ourselves. In some cases, if we could not
do this, we would go stark, raving mad of frustration, for there are
times when there is nowhere to go but to God. However, for every
person who is frustrated because of what he has tried to do and can't
do, there are probably hundreds who haven't begun to do what they
could do. Nobody has any right to feel frustrated about anything
until he has personally used his meantime right up to the limit. And
it is my personal conviction that God would be more likely to welcome
our falling back upon him if it were from exhaustion. That would
be more convincing than languidly praying, "I say, God, would you
terribly much mind doing what I don't personally care enough about
to do myself?"

A lot of us are still at the "God, bless all the hungry people and give
them enough to eat" stage. Giving them enough to eat will probably
take some money. More than that, it will probably take some sacrificial effort. More than that, it may take some organized, legislated,
joint effort. If, as some church people seem to think, "legislation"
is unchristian, perhaps the question is: How big must an effort be
before it becomes unchristian, or how small must it be to remain
Christian? Is it more Christian to give a hungry man a quarter or
a dollar for something to eat than to vote for a Congressman who
has a sense of legislative compassion? Or is "the meantime" big
enough to accommodate both acts of mercy?

It should be pointed out here that it is entirely possible to use a
substandard meantime as a prison into which to lock those we should
and could be setting at liberty. Being able to give a quarter or a
dollar is worth more than the cost of giving it. To be a benefactor
means there must be somebody in need of benefaction. Though presumably we will never run out of worthy causes, it's somehow more

delicious to contribute to the alleviation of need than to remove the occasion of need. To do the latter, you must somehow get the needy person at least up to a reasonable level of competence and affluence. I am almost afraid to wonder whether there will not be needy people in the world as long as there are other people who will be made to feel good by throwing crumbs to them. But of this I am sure: even in our philanthropy we are reluctant to surrender the delights of superiority.

It's in real life almost as it was when I was a small boy and had the idea one summer day of starting a hospital for butterflies. I fixed up a wooden box with a wire-screen front, and when I had my hospital ready, I went out with a stick and batted down some butter-flies for patients. In the meantime, those battered butterflies no doubt needed a quiet place in which to recuperate, but it was I who had created their meantime for them. If today we are not creating some of the world's meantimes, the possibility is that we are at least main-taining them in some sense, exacting a recompense in grumbling that enhances rather than diminishes our personal pride.

There are all sorts of meantimes which, if we could, we would wish to escape. There are those people who are waiting for an inspiration to do something great. But in the meantime, life goes on, and what they hoped to do by inspiration (that is, without drudgery) doesn't get done. There are those who are waiting for some incontrovertible, ultimate truth to hit them like a ton of bricks. But in the meantime, they have to live as if *something* is true. Even if they try not to, they are, in the very humdrum processes of living, betting their lives on something. To say that they believe nothing, accept nothing, pending their final determination of truth, is nonsense. Nobody can escape his meantime—either by taking refuge in a religious hiding place or in a nonreligious hiding place.

There are those who are waiting to go somewhere, to read a par-ticular book, to explore an idea, to cultivate a new hobby, to become a new person. Often these potential interests are put off until old age. "When I retire, then I'm going to . . ." prefaces a multitude of lost causes. Postponement—even for the best of reasons—becomes a habit,

I suspect, and once a habit is well-learned, it is hard to break. How sad to let a life full of meantime go down the drain.

Not only by default or through indifference or through procrastination do we fail to live in the only place where living can be done—the present—but sometimes the very prospect of being alive terrifies us or seems immensely impractical. It is much easier to be religious in terms of passively believing that Christ will someday, somehow, rule the world, fill all dinner buckets, solve all problems, wipe away all tears, than to be Christlike in those areas ourselves. We've let ourselves act as if we believe that faith just doesn't really work where life is real and earnest—in, say, politics or business. We support with investment and purchase dollars the very things we said in church on Sunday that we didn't believe in. Righteousness, justice, is something you do only if other things are equal. Christianity is great for the theoretical underpinnings, but watch it when anyone tries to talk you into applying those theories to a given situation—that's where you get into trouble. Keep it nicely fuzzy and future, and it won't get in anybody's way.

The people who reason thus—and we all turn out to have the most amazing blind spots—are committing their lives not to Christ but to whoever is paying the top interest rate. Things like descending from heaven with a shout or the life-everlasting-amen, we're quite willing to concede to Christ's jurisdiction. But in the meantime, don't try to read religion into the size and number of rats in my city's slums, or a teen-ager dying of heroin, or what goes on in the nearby prison.

We deny so regularly with our meantimes what we affirm with our eternities. And we don't even realize we are doing it.

The difficulty with waiting around for something to start is that when it does, it's hard to put your finger on it and say, "Now! It's starting!" Does a vacation start when the car is finally packed and everybody is inside and the doors are slammed and the seat belts are fastened and the motor is started and you back out of the driveway? Does it start as you turn down the street? Does it start when you arrive at the cottage on the beach? Does it start when you get into your bathing suit and rush to the water for the first plunge? When does—or did—it start? If we wait for an indisputable signal, will it ever come? In the meantime. . . .

Of course, you have long-range goals. You're looking forward to the day when the children will be grown, or the Democrats or Republicans are in or out, or the streets are safe, or life is less bewildering. But in the meantime . . .?

In the meantime, the message that got through to bewildered, unhappy, needy, blind Bartimaeus, sitting by the dusty roadside contemplating his woes, when he heard that Jesus was passing by, may have something to say to us: "Take heart; rise, he is calling you."

But, you may very well say, Jesus doesn't happen to be coming down my street, and the chances of his calling me to do anything are pretty slim.

Which is where prayer, one of the most misused resources of life, comes in.

14) Prayer as more than room service

There's something exquisitely luxurious about room service in a hotel. All you have to do is pick up the phone and somebody is ready and waiting to bring you breakfast, lunch, dinner, chocolate milkshake, whatever your heart desires and your stomach will tolerate. Or by another languid motion of the wrist, you can telephone for someone who will get a soiled shirt quickly transformed into a clean one or a rumpled suit into a pressed one.

That's the concept that some of us have of prayer. We have created God in the image of a divine bellhop. Prayer, for us, is the ultimate in room service, wrought by direct dialing. Furthermore, no tipping, and everything charged to that great credit card in the sky.

Now, prayer is many things, but I'm pretty sure this is not one of the things it is. I do not claim to understand the techniques of the "great men of prayer," as they have been called, or even to know for sure what was and is meant by that awe-filled designation. What I am rather certain about is that, as we do with such efficient alacrity in matters of faith, we have turned the tables, snarled the guidelines, switched the priorities. We've promoted prayer as a self-serving jiffy gadget for twisting God's arm, a soul-sized Aladdin's lamp— or, equally blasphemous, as a stern Christian duty that may not be much fun but is somewhere piling up Brownie points to our account. What a joyless faith that regards prayer as a life sentence, the onerous price of admission to the club! And what a faithless faith that thinks of prayer as negotiable special privilege ("I thank thee, that I am not as other men are").

There are some other things that prayer is not:

Prayer is not a way to lobby in the halls of heaven.

Prayer is not a let-God-do-it means of evading responsibilities which are rightfully our own.

Prayer is not a means by which we can persuade God to do what he does not very much wish to do.

Prayer is not even a means by which God must be urged to do what is his nature to do.

Prayer is not a lever which we may use to bend God's will to our will.

Prayer is not a bulletin by which we must inform God of current news, and without which he is uninformed. (There was the seminary professor who opened his classes with prayer, invariably prefaced by, "O God, as thou didst see in the *New York Times* this morning. . . .")

But see what prayer is:

A means by which we allow God to persuade us to do what *we* do not very much wish to do.

A means by which we let God do through *us* what is his nature to do.

An available lever for the bending of *our* will to God's will.
A way to sensitize our souls to the needs of others.
Strength for the shouldering of our responsibilities.
And, most of all, prayer is the assurance of presence.

That last makes me think of the uneasy nights I spent as a small boy. That house in which we lived on the side of one of Pittsburgh's hills was three stories high in the front and four in the back. The bottom layer was the cellar and the top was what we called the third floor, really a finished attic, the ceiling of which was cut into shadowed geometric shapes by dormer windows. Up there were two bedrooms, a hallway, and a mysterious storage room for trunks that always smelled of mothballs and history. Our family slept there, because the second floor was usually rented out to a "tenant" to help pay the rent. Being the youngest, I had to go to bed first, and it was a long way up all those steps. My father usually came with me, for we didn't have electricity above the second floor and the gas light had to be turned on, and then off when I was tucked in.

That bed in that room on the third floor seemed to be at the ends of the earth, remote from human habitation, close to unexplained noises and dark secrets. At my urging, my father would try to stop the windows from rattling, wedging wooden matchsticks into the cracks. But they always rattled in spite of his efforts. Sometimes he would read me a story, but inevitably the time came when he would turn out the light and shut the door and I would hear his steps on the stairs, growing fainter. Then all would be quiet, except for the rattling windows and my cowering imagination.

Once, I remember, my father said, "Would you rather I leave the light on and go downstairs, or turn the light out and stay with you for awhile?" You can guess that I chose presence with darkness, over absence with light.

Is that not what we really want most when we pray—the assurance that Someone is there? And if Someone is, darkness or light does not matter. Somehow, presence has gone out of prayer, and when this goes, nothing much is left.

A friend told me once about something his son, then also a small boy, said, and it became for me a discernment to remember. It was night and his mother had asked him to put the empty milk bottles out on the porch so they would be ready for the milkman in the morning. The boy took the bottles, opened the door, and looked out into the pitch blackness. Turning, he hesitated and said, "It's too dark to go out without a father."

Prayer is not an asking license. It is presence—in sickness and in health, for better and for worse.

But what about the verse that promises, "Whatsoever ye shall ask in my name, that will I do"? Of course, but don't miss the fine print: "in my name." That means a lot more than the open-sesame status we have given it. Tacking on some variation of the words at the end of a prayer, simply as a validation or a trinitarian imprimatur or a visa stamp that moves you promptly along to the window that's handing out the goodies is a demeaning concept. To pray "in my name" calls for a prayer that Jesus himself might pray, which is a cut or two above asking for a Flexible Flyer or the adult equivalent. To pray in Jesus' name means to pray in his spirit, in his compassion, in his love, in his outrage, in his concern. And that requires, first of all, a sense of presence of God—and of man.

For you cannot get beyond even the first word of the prayer that Jesus offered as a model without finding a brother and taking him with you the rest of the way: "*Our* Father." That was what was wrong with the Pharisee's prayer—there was no "our" in it; it was all "I."

When one begins to sense that prayer is presence, not room service, some other things begin to fall in line. For one, prayer becomes something essentially basic. We have complicated and profaned it with attempts to work up a sweat, "agonizing," some people call it. One may well have profound, shattering experiences in prayer, but I often get the feeling that we tend to agonize best before an audience of our peers. We have profaned prayer, I think, by trying to organize it, program it, formalize it, ritualize it. We try to get whole churches or cities or nations praying at the same time and preferably for the same thing, as if we were setting up a picket line to bring our grievances to God's attention or waging a cosmic protest. It is no doubt true that there are immense psychological values in getting large numbers of people to pray for the same thing. But is it any more Christian to use prayer to try to manipulate people than to use it to try to manipulate God? And is God any more likely to be impressed with wholesale prayer than retail, or with round-the-clock prayer marathons than with unpremeditated moments when his presence evokes an impulsive thank you? Again, of course, the psychological effects of the mass effort may be tremendous, if you happen to go for prayer as exploitation.

We've made prayer into such a hygienic, hands-off procedure. We pray, and think we can stay out of whatever the trouble is. Prayer is the way into trouble. It is life-changing, and the life it changes most is your own. You cannot pray with clenched fists. You cannot pray long without committing yourself to what you're praying for.

Prayer is of course much more than all this. Who can fully describe or practice its power? Where the end of its power is, I do not know. But of this I am convinced: the beginning of the power of prayer is not, "Lord, give something to me." It is, rather, "Lord, give me to something."

And it's simple. No secret efficacious words, even though some people seem to think you must take a Berlitz course in Conversational Prayer before you dare talk to God.

I remember having lunch with a naval commander who, at retirement, was about to become a kind of technological missionary in Southeast Asia. His views were perhaps influenced by the fact that the language of the country to which he was going and which he would have to learn had some half-dozen variations of the word used for direct address, depending upon the social station of the one to whom you were speaking, so that you had to know almost a man's whole history before you could even say hello. Anyway, when I happened to mention my secret preference for "You" as against "Thou" in public prayer, he was aghast. In his opinion, God deserved better treatment then that, some form of address different from and superior to that which we accord others.

When we give the impression that God may be suitably addressed only in a certain kind of language, we are, I think, guilty of introducing a crippling degree of self-consciousness into our praying. Inability to pray certainly doesn't stem from having nothing to say. Often it does stem from thinking you have to say it in what amounts to a foreign tongue. Traditional prayer-talk is unlike anything else that one will encounter outside the King James version of the Bible and perhaps the hymnbook. While we have been always exhorted to translate our faith into everyday concerns and deeds, and when the Bible has been translated into numerous modern English versions, we have not yet been adequately encouraged to translate our prayers.

What did people do for thees and thous and wilts and wasts and dosts in their prayers before the era of "holy" King James English? The King James translation of the Bible was made in 1611, but prayers were being said long before that, and we may safely assume that they were reasonably devout ones. The fine print of the flowery dedication of my King James Bible says that here is "one more exact Translation of the Holy Scriptures into the English Tongue." It was not translated into the language of special holiness, but into the language of the people.

How much it—the source of so much of our prayer vocabulary— was the language of the people I did not realize until I opened a ponderous unabridged dictionary to the word "thou." What it had to say was absolutely shattering: "*Thou*—used in Middle English and in early modern English at least into the 17th century as the appropriate form of address to an intimate friend or a person of lower social status than the speaker."

And here we moderns thought we were being holy when we were really being profane!

Prayer is and ought to be the most natural thing in the world.

For some, that will mean using every dost and wast that can be mustered. For others, the reassurance that one word is no holier than another may provide liberation that will make prayer not only meaningful but indispensable. We don't *have* to force ourselves into somebody else's mold. If we could just grasp that one idea!

15) God, that I may lose my cool!

Webster and I and other back numbers think that "cool" makes a better adjective than noun. But as used today, it's sometimes a noun that stands in a sentence by itself, neither modified nor modifying. Cool is something you are, something you have. Cool is what you do and, more particularly, what you don't do. Cool is more than emotional temperature. It is a way of thinking, a way of living, a way of being.

Cool goes further than blush-deep. It has to do with total composure, aloofness, uninvolvement. It's not a mask behind which to seethe unseen. If you have cool, you don't seethe. There's nothing worth getting that perturbed about, nothing worth losing yourself in. Being caught with ulcers would be the supreme humiliation for one who has cool.

Marshall McLuhan, the Canadian professor who lectures about communication, I think means something else by cool and hot, but since I am not sure what he does mean, I won't get into that. Nor into hot and cold in the Laodicean sense, which is another story.

I'm not talking, either, about cool in the sense of not bothering to call the cops when you hear somebody being pummeled to death outside your home. The most tempting kind of cool for me is the kind being peddled in the best of neighborhoods and churches where I am continually advised in one way or another, "Don't get excited!"

What I want to know is, why shouldn't I get excited? What was ever accomplished by unexcited people? As nearly as I can tell, more things are wrought by enthusiasm than this world dreams of. And though Newton might have been sitting around when he observed an apple falling from a tree, I daresay he developed quite an interest in apples before he came up with the Law of Gravity, which is still being generally obeyed today. On this matter of enthusiasm, someone has well said, "If you can keep your head while all about are losing theirs, you just don't understand how serious the situation is." Or, you may not want to understand. Or, you may not allow yourself to understand. Because when you understand, you have to commit yourself, give yourself, and we don't much like to do that any more. Clergy and laity alike, we'd rather be bleacher preachers—egging somebody else on to do what we ourselves are not excited enough to do.

And when you get right down to it, men and women who have lost their cool are not the most popular people in the crowd. We call them radicals, fanatics, nuts. We like them better dead than alive, for when they've passed on—with or without assistance— and we're enjoying the fruits of their commitment, we build monuments to them.

The rest of us try to keep every emotion air-conditioned, sterile, untouched by human hearts (at least by ours). We take refuge behind the doors of homes and churches and offices, and if all else fails, we hide behind words, which is one of the best hiding places there is. We can talk all around a subject, prodding it here and there, without ever revealing ourselves. We don't vote yes and we don't vote no. We just don't vote—usually for the announced reason that we don't have enough information to make a decision, which is cool for "As long as I don't make up my mind, it won't cost me anything."

Where, I wonder, are the people who are willing to see something through or who think that anything is worth seeing through? In business or in marriage or in any relationship you see whole strings of unburned bridges behind. You see people going through life without ever sitting deep in the saddle. And how, I wonder, can you ever make much of anything, most of all a life, that you don't have a stake in? Where is the risk capital for a new world coming from?

No, we don't want to lose our cool. Not anywhere. Have you noticed how, when you have a group of friends in of an evening, or a discussion gets going in a church meeting, and there's any disagreement, somebody quickly tries to reconcile the viewpoints? "Now, you both believe this much . . ." says the arbitrator, as if he were negotiating a labor contract. If the parties leave on other than common ground, we all feel vaguely uncomfortable. But why do we *have* to agree about everything? Why *not* go away mad? A lot of people have gone far because they were mad—William Carey, pioneer of modern missions, for one. Somebody had told him to sit down, that when God wanted to convert "the heathen" he'd do it singlehanded. Can't you just picture today's arbitrator-type getting those two together? "Now, you are both agreed, are you not, that *somebody* must convert them?" And by the time Carey got out of that session, he would have decided that shoemaking was not such a bad trade and there was really nothing to get excited about.

Consensus, it seems to me, never gets anybody anywhere. All it does is show where people already are. The challenge is in doing something that hasn't been done, in thinking what hasn't been thought, in giving what hasn't been given, of cutting oneself out from the herd. "I know not what others may do, *but as for me. . . .*" To say it is to shatter your cool to smithereens.

The unpardonable sin these days seems to be to speak up in meeting, to speak out in conversation, to express a conviction, to take a stand, to reveal yourself. Church ought to be the best place of all in which we can say precisely what we think about anything and be confident that everything we say will be used *for* us. There, the thirteenth chapter of I Corinthians should be in force as nowhere else.

Well, we may not have perfect love in church, but we have perfect cool. Somebody could make a fortune selling to congregations the sign you sometimes see in barbershops: "We do not discuss politics or religion." Nothing will be said to disturb you.

Oh, we come up with answers in the cool way the Apostles responded to the question, "Who do men say that I, the son of man, am?" But who dares now to ask—or answer—the question, "Who do *you* say that I am?"

The hard truth is that we have let cool, detached, objective, look-at-it-from-all-sides neutralism take the place of passionate deed. We got the Post Office to print, "Pray for Peace" on the mail, and figured the job was done whether anybody prayed or worked for peace or not. It wasn't. In fact, when anybody took it seriously, we indignantly called him a "Peacenik." We manage to get "In God We Trust" printed on dollar bills and think we have delivered a mortal blow to the powers of darkness. You can hear some very eloquent theorizing in pulpit and pew these days. But who is laying his life on the line for what he says he believes? Who cares enough to give the very best—namely, himself. There are notable exceptions.

Somebody in this world has to play it hot. Somebody has to do something, not just look on bemusedly. In your church, somebody is playing it hot, or there wouldn't be a church in which anybody else could keep his cool. Most of us are on the sidewalk, waiting for the parade. So who's marching? We've got blessings to burn—comfortable buildings, comfortable furnishings, comfortable music—and a sit-in faith. Sure, we're getting our money's worth. The trouble is, it isn't supposed to be that way. Somebody else should be getting our money's worth. That's what the Christian life is all about.

Instead, we're hoarders—of money, yes, but mostly of emotions, of reactions. We think we can spend our lives or not, when actually we're spending them willy-nilly, if only to buy standing time on a streetcorner. Wouldn't it be smarter—and more fun—to spend them deliberately, consciously, intentionally for something worth such a price?

Even in religion—perhaps especially in religion—we expect things to be cool, contained, orderly, predictable, detached. Yet Edison's observation is as applicable here as anywhere else: "Genius is 1 per cent inspiration and 99 per cent perspiration." This goes for the genius of faith, too. And yet, those who have their cool, in church and out, insist, "No sweat."

We want the angels without the sheep, the baby without the birth, the Christ without the Jesus, the redemption without the Cross, the gain without the risk, the finding without the losing, the love without the hurt.

Are you looking for a prayer to pray? Try this one: "God, that I may lose my cool!"

16) Sweat on the upper lip

But there are some people who are so heavy-handed, heavy-footed, heavy-souled when they get hot! I am thinking especially of the lapel-grabbing type who gets right up in your face with his appalling earnestness. (What a job Durer could do on *these* "Preying Hands"!) If he ever laughs, it must be in a dark corner somewhere when no one is watching. Ideas, to him, are something you transmit by brute force. He doesn't trust his ideas enough to let them go anywhere unaccompanied. Perhaps, in fact, this is because they are not *his* ideas at all, but somebody else's over which he presumes he has been appointed guardian.

These super-earnest types make me nervous, for I always think they are trying to put something over on me. They want me to look at them, nowhere else; hear them, no one else; and I wonder what I should be seeing or hearing somewhere else. This kind of thing makes me especially nervous when religion is involved. I give my allegiance and undivided ear very reluctantly to anybody who has perspiration on his upper lip. This is frankly my quarrel with some of the new sects. They are growing, I understand, but I want them to do their growing somewhere else than in my living room. That goes for anyone who is so dead earnest about anything pertaining to God and man that he cannot see a certain ludicrousness in his own presumption to omniscience. The "dead" in "dead earnest" is more than a semantic coincidence. No one is fully alive who has a closed mind, and it has to be closed, solidified, ossified, petrified (as by fear) for terminal earnestness to set in. The paradox is that when in this connection we use the word "dead" we should unwittingly be so accurate.

If there is anything that can put a crimp in the lapel-grabbing industry it is a slight touch of nonomniscience. There is certainly enough of it to go around. For all we can think about deity, a J. B. Phillips can still say with justification, "Your God is too small." Any God we could pin down with a definition would be pin-sized. If we could say *exactly* what he is, how he operates, what he thinks, we would be his peers, not his creation. When faith becomes utterly scrutable, it has ceased to be faith.

The thing that disturbs me most about people who think they have all the answers is that this turns them into closed corporations, and, if pursued, into non-Christian ones. It would be vexing, I should think, to live with omniscience. It is even more vexing to live with *presumed* omniscience, as any number of wives and husbands (and children and parents) can testify. One of the facts of life is the mystery, the mystique of life—the unanswered questions, the apparent bafflements and contradictions. Something there is in us that doesn't love a loose end, and we seize all sorts of justifications for tying them up. Quoting chapter and verse, or creedal statement, or the faith of our fathers and grandfathers, we go about frantically applying tourniquets that not only stop the bleeding but threaten the flow of life itself. Ultimate earnestness, focused to a searing, blinding light, is completely ruthless. Conviction, concern, sincerity, *earnestness* are meant to warm the beholder, not to incinerate him.

The only way, I submit, to keep earnestness in the asset column is to mix it with humor. Unfortunately, humor has not yet been fully accepted into the Christian canon—it's one of the apocryphal virtues. Perhaps this is because it is such an instant solvent for pomp and pretense. It has a way of cutting presumption down to size, and presumption has more nerve endings per square inch than any other part of our psychic anatomy.

I spoke of mixing humor with earnestness, but it is more than that. It's not so much a mixture of two components as a compound that is something more than the sum of the parts. Humor at best is of the essence of earnestness and of life. It is a way of looking at everything through eyes that have laugh crinkles at the corners. It is the knack of seeing humor in what we do and what we are, not of *using* it for any purpose, however good. "Humorous" is not an adjective but an attitude. It's not something you say, but a posture of mind. Humor, essentially, is humility, and perhaps that is why it is unpopular in religious circles, where humility does not come easily.

I'm not talking, you understand, about *jokes,* or advocating that the preacher get off a bully one at the start of the sermon in order to capture the attention of the audience. Such jokes are often colossal embarrassments to pulpit and pew—the speaker feeling that now he has got that out of the way he can get down to business (or worse, can explain its spiritual implications), and the audience, that it has now left the oasis behind. Real humor doesn't have to make a point. It's just *there*, bubbling up like a spring that flows whether anybody comes for water or not. One may not even necessarily get very many chortles out of the person who does that kind of bubbling. All you may sense is that here is somebody who does not think of himself more highly than he ought to think and that you are more open, more genuine when you're with him.

One of the reasons we've been so wary of humor is that we were handed down a pretty grim, unsmiling sort of faith. Even the word "Protestant"—one who protests—is an unsmiling word; its defenses are up and it's breathing hard before anybody has said anything.

Another part of the reason for locking humor out of our faith probably goes back to the Bible. Look up the word "laugh" or "laughter" in a concordance, and you get the notion that mirth is not one of the spiritual gifts most to be sought after. Biblical laughter runs to pretty cynical stuff—Sarah laughing at God, God laughing in derision, somebody laughing someone "to scorn," the righteous having a last laugh on the unrighteous.

I think we've been looking under the wrong word for our biblical cues on humor. A much better word than "laughter" would be "joy," and the Bible has a great deal—all of it good—to say about that. Joy, for my money, shatters pomposity and pride, it bubbles, is never heavy-handed, and is simply another name for the best kind of humor.

Which brings us to the last barrier that remains to be cracked. Despite our mighty-fortress approach to faith (immobility and security vs. mobility and risk), we have acquired a certain confidence in getting out among people and mingling. We're not quite as frightened of "the world" as we used to be. We've discovered that we don't care if the saints *are* watching—when we see something that tickles our funnybone, we laugh, and find ourselves enjoying it more. But we have not yet learned to be truly joyful, bubbly, bouncy about the things that matter most to us—namely, those things pertaining to ourselves and to God. Try for yourself looking into a mirror and laughing. It's not easy! We are still seeing through the glass darkly—very darkly. We think that *we, our* institutions, *our* church, *our* God are utterly deadpan contemplations. God himself must smile at *that*, and wish that we too felt secure enough to smile.

Humor will never destroy anything that is genuine. All it can do is puncture balloons. Only when humor is regarded as betrayal and joy as treason, is the church in real trouble. In this complicated, disturbing, revolutionary period of history, five senses are just not enough. We need two more: a sense of compassion and a sense of humor. And it seems to me that they go together.

Both relate to life-style, personality. They are deep-down, welling-up traits, if they are genuine. Jesus put it: "The words that the mouth utters come from the overflowing of the heart. A good man produces good from the store of good within himself." (Matt. 12:34-35, *New English Bible*). The priority, it seems to me, is first the storehouse, then the merchandise.

17) "What can I do?" may be the phony question

There are, I will readily concede, times and places in which the question is a real and useful one. A pastor or a Sunday school superintendent, for example, would feel his heart strangely warmed, should the question be put to him. And a busy mother would no doubt react with incredulous delight, should her teen-age offspring troop to the kitchen after Sunday dinner to present the question to the lady with her hands in the dishwater.

But there is something about this question that deserves a second listen. It's being asked more and more often when any problem comes up anywhere about anything. I'm getting the feeling that many times it's not the question that should be evoked, and that what we are often looking for is something we can go out and "do" and get over with and so get off some hook or other. Certainly it's not the first question to ask.

If it's starving children, we want to get in there and feed them so those pictures of hunger-swollen bellies won't nag our consciences. Having paid our dollar, we can then go about our business. If it's the ghetto, O.K., we go in with a can of paint and a shovel, clean it up, and we've done our part. If it's the Sunday dishes, we get a virtuous glow out of all proportion to the fact that during the year this was one batch of dishes out of approximately 1,000.

Not that the feeding doesn't have to be done and the dollars paid and the volunteer labor shared and the classes taught and the den mothers found and the canvassers enlisted and all the rest. But why it is that you find the *same* people doing so many of the world's housekeeping chores that have to be done? And generally pitching in without having to ask, "What can I do?" I think this relates to the fact that "What can I do?" isn't the basic question at all.

The basic question is, "What can I *be*?"

Being takes a lot more effort than doing, for you're never finished with it. And when you start out with the premise of *being* something, the doing naturally follows, with considerably more perception and considerably less grumbling and foot-dragging. Because then, doing is the logical follow-through. If you're committed to love, your love will make itself known in all sorts of ways that an unloving person couldn't imagine and certainly couldn't program. If you are committed to compassion, you recognize opportunities to use it that you would never have seen if you had simply gone out looking for something to "do."

It's my growing conviction that some stupid and clumsy things are being done in this world simply because people have the compulsion to "do" something and yet are not deeply enough committed to "be" something.

I've heard speakers who were asked, after a presentation on narcotics or hunger or war or racial tension or the Middle East or suffering of one kind or another, "What can I do?" and who were somewhat embarrassed by not knowing quite what to answer. Some of them frankly admitted that they didn't know what the listener could do. Some of the problems of life are so complex, so tightly entwined with other problems, that it's difficult to pull out one strand and "solve" that one all by itself. Some problems have to be dealt with on several fronts at once, if the situation is to improve. And some of the fronts may not happen to interest you or me very much, or may be too close to home for comfort. Getting at that kind of problem takes much more than "doing" something at a safe distance.

It takes *being* something—and probably something that we never have been and never thought we could or would be.

This kind of reaction calls for no less than a total personal revolution. It's utterly radical—the kind of experience Jesus was talking about when he used the shattering expression "born again." We've allowed that revolutionary concept of personality transformation to become a namby-pamby "spiritual" concept, a sort of religious joke. Try such a cataclysmic reordering of priorities on the stock market, for example, and it won't look so namby-pamby. Try this radical kind of "being" in politics and see what happens. Lay it alongside the graph that shows how your tax money is spent. See what it has to do with the kind of car you buy—or whether you buy one at all this year.

Most of us won't have to face any of those dilemmas, for it's easier to do than to be. And when there doesn't seem to be anything we can do, we feel frustrated, cheated. "Why doesn't somebody let me do something, so I can get out from under this sense that things are wrong and my world is caving in?"

Starting at that end, if we were told, would we do it anyway? Remember the rich young ruler who once came to Jesus? His question was the same as our plaintive "What can I do?" He asked, "What good thing shall I do that I may inherit eternal life?" Which is exactly the same as our question. That's what we want—to look good, to do the right thing, to be remembered, to get all that's coming to us. Except that maybe today we've pulled in our question so that it barely covers life here, let alone hereafter. What can I do to hold things together until I'm on Social Security, or until the children are through college, or to make sure that my church stays alive and vigorous through this decade?

How rich, actually, was a rich young ruler then? Ever thought of that? Just inventory the things you have today that all the wealth in the world couldn't have bought him. Radio. Television. Central heating. Air conditioning. Foods from all over the world. Regular meals. Dependable—more or less—transportation. We're richer than he was! And we know how well off we are, you'd better believe it! That's why, when we start with his question today, we come up with his response.

For, of course, when Jesus told him what to do, he didn't do it. Neither do we. We'll just not get off the ground, or get anybody else off the ground, by asking, or trying to answer, the empty, inadequate, phony question, "What can I do?" For the real question is, "What can I be?" And when you're ready to be something, become excited about being something, the cost is manageable.

The remarkable thing about all this is that the be-ers turn out invariably to be the doers. A do-in has no staying power. It comes and goes. Maybe it will accomplish something as it flashes by, but it won't change the world because it doesn't want to be bothered with root causes. The world is changed by those who care enough to give themselves, not those who merely lend themselves.

You can't easily get candidates for a particular sacrifice. I'm very suspicious of the person who mounts a soapbox and proclaims, "I'm ready to die for my country!" for I don't see him doing much of it. Or to die for Christianity. Or freedom. Or integrity. For you don't go into total commitment with an itemized pledge of what you're prepared to do. You go into it only with a determination of what you're prepared to be. Once you're over that hurdle, you have a vastly different idea about what is expensive and what is not, about the use of possessions, about what is a bargain and what isn't.

I remember a former missionary telling about his "insurance policies." He had not put a great deal of money into life insurance that would some day provide funds for his children. "I am putting my money into mission projects," he said. "I think that is better insurance for the future of the world and therefore of my children."

You couldn't tell someone to go out and "do" that. It wouldn't make sense. To this man, who had given years of life in the Philippines and had been interned with his family in a Japanese prison camp, it didn't make sense not to do it.

When we ask, "What can I do?" do we really want to know? I am sure that some of us really do. God can use even our inadvertence, our inadequacies and our stumbling steps to get us to where we should go.

But the more probing, revealing, responsive question is "What can I be?"

When are we going to get around to asking that one—and listening for an answer? Do we care that much about the way things are—and what they, and we, could become?

18) There are some things we can't love our way out of

You'll find love on just about any Christian's list of qualities to be cultivated. Probably never before have so many people had so much to say about love. When there's so much talk about a topic, there are bound to be a few blurred edges.

Of course, it all depends upon what you mean by love. I have the feeling that what we most often mean is a long way from what love really is. And I am not thinking of love in the sense of *eros*, the sexy member of the trio of Greek words for love that ministers trot out when they preach sermons on loving. *Eros*, whatever else may be right or wrong with it—and from the pulpit it is treated rather too disdainfully, I think—doesn't lack for being pretty well understood for what it is, even if nobody gets all that specific. The other two, the kinds of love Christians are most outspoken about—*phileo* and *agape*—are the "spiritual" ones of the trio, and the greater of these is agape, self-giving, unmerited love. These two are the ones we have promoted (eros didn't seem to require much promotion) and have also perverted.

Where we got into trouble was trying to use this high-level kind of love for our own purposes. We did it, unconsciously perhaps, because it looked like an easy way out. It would save us a lot of trouble. We wouldn't have to inconvenience ourselves, change our habits or our traditions, correct injustice, lay out any money, get the least bit upset about anything. All we had to do was *love*. You could love from a distance, not so much as getting your hands dirty or your mind disturbed. It was all so hygienic. We were glad Jesus thought of it and made it the basis of our relationship to God and to man. For all we had to do was love a nice rosy glow right over anything that was unpleasant. Love was guaranteed to cover in one coat. Love everybody, and everything will be all right. I'm going to bestow my love upon you—lucky you! This is what we were led to believe.

But we were never led to believe it by Jesus. As we have done with so many of the things he said, we put a halo over the words, took them out of the context of life, built a nice little shrine around them. It just never occurred to us that love is more than a warm glow, a kindly feeling. We liked it because we assumed it didn't cost anything.

How wrong can you get? Love, far from being cheap, is the most costly commodity in the world. Jesus knew it all along and we just didn't get the point, even after he proved it one Friday.

There are any number of examples, but race relations is a perfect one. The word went out, "Love blacks," as it had been going out for generations, "Love whites." And whites began loving for all they were worth. They fairly oozed love. They thought love, vibrated love. The Bible said, "Love your neighbor," and so they tried. They really tried. From white pulpit and pew the word went out, "We love you, boy." And then they sat back, exhausted by all this outpouring of good will. But tension mounted, relationships deteriorated. There was talk about Black Power and whites got all nervous—though White Power had never given them any concern, or Methodist Power or Baptist Power or Republican Power or Democratic Power.

"Maybe we didn't love hard enough," whites thought, and shut their eyes and vibrated love some more. But when they opened them, nothing had changed except for the worse. They began to wonder if this love thing was all it was cracked up to be. They began to wonder even more, and some whites were utterly baffled, when they heard blacks say, "We don't care whether you love us or not. What we want is justice!"

And that puts the finger right on the sore spot. Love—genuine, Jesus-type love—is not something you *think* but something you *do*. Love is not closed eyes, but open eyes. Love is not a warm spirit but sore feet. Love is not being gloriously safe but terribly vulnerable. Love is not cool but hot. Love is not for hallowing enshrined wrongs but for routing and righting wrongs. Love is not a sentimental word but a demanding way of life; it insists that our feet, our hands, our minds, our goals, our treasure be where our heart is.

What a dainty dogma we have made of loving! No wonder so many people, observing the unscarred hands of the church, have been passing by on the other side. Some of these "non-believers" knew us better than we knew ourselves. They knew that we thought all we had to do was love until it hurt and then quit, when actually we had not even begun to love until it hurt.

Talk about relevance! Get into some real, honest-to-goodness loving, and you'll find you are where the action is. And you won't be where the action is and you won't know what love is until you have made a down payment with a piece of your life as security.

We sing so lightheartedly, "Love so amazing, so divine, demands my soul, my life, my all," meaning that Christ's love demands them—which is true, though I think that "commands" would be a better word there. *My* love, however, indisputably *demands* my soul, my life, my all. Our mistake has been in thinking that our love didn't demand anything more than the announcing of it.

We thought love would hide a multitude of sins. It didn't, and it doesn't. We wanted to be so sure of the purity of our motivation that we took the verse, "Though I bestow all my goods to feed the poor . . . and have not love, it profiteth me nothing," and made it read, "If I have love, bestowing my goods profits me nothing." Come to think about it, part of the blame for our misconceptions about the material rewards of love may stem from that very King

James phraseology, considering the way we rise to the profit motive. It's less commercial in *The New English Bible*: ". . . if I have no love, I am none the better" (or our twisted corollary, "If I have love, and do not . . . I am none the worse."). Those who are doing *and* loving are making both their loving and their doing meaningful.

There is something else that ought to be said about our strange idea of what love is. That is, the futility of trying to love people in category lots. For several years now, it has been drummed into us, "Love the black race." "Love the white race." How, in the name of common sense, can you love a *race*? Or a nationality? Or Jews? Or Catholics? Or, for that matter, Protestants? (How can you even *hate* a category?) Yet this wraparound love, this love in the abstract, was the big thing. And when we ran into those who were unlovable—which we do all the time—thinking we were bound by Holy Writ to love them anyway, we felt guilty.

There is a certain theological sense in which love (agape) must be across-the-board, without favoritism. But even Jesus chose twelve out of the multitude. Call that what you will, a focused love, rapport, whatever. I submit that you can't love—in the sense of having rapport—a *category*. You can love only *individuals*. And it follows that some individuals—of any race, color or creed, including my own—are going to irritate me, in the sense of producing violent nonrapport. My wraparound love comes in, not at the point of spirit communing with spirit, but at the point of my active belief in justice for all, my respect for the human dignity of all persons, whether I know them intimately or not, whether I like them or not. *That* is the only kind of generalized, wraparound love that makes sense. And once we're giving that kind of love (and there's a certain presumption even in the notion that it's ours to give!), then we—all of us— can begin narrowing our focus, finding the individuals with whom we can share ideas, theirs and ours. Or we can then be open to their finding us. For it may well be that we shall not have our own twelve, but be one of somebody else's twelve—and there is no law that says that this somebody has to be of our own race.

I think it's significant that Jesus said—and let's not forget that

he, a Jew, got it out of Leviticus—"Love thy neighbor as thyself."
He then told a story to explain who a man's neighbor was. The
neighbor could be found wherever there were hurts to be healed,
wrongs to be righted, pains to be felt. He was saying that I find
my neighbor by what I *do*, not in my grandiose resolves. And he
didn't say "neighbors," plural. He made it very singular, very personal, as personal as I myself am personal.

When he did use the plural—"Love your enemies"—it was more
personal than the faceless "the enemy" that military people are prone
to talk about. *Your enemies.* How many do *you* have? Not so many,
chances are, that you can't count them. Not so many that you can't
love them.

And, there, too, the beginning of love is justice. And the beginning
of justice is the sobering reflection that I violate any man's personhood at my peril. If I violate him while I say I love him—or, shame
of shames, *because* I love him—I have never learned the first thing
about what love is.

19) Would you believe Noah and a chicken in a rowboat?

To have faith without fear, you sooner or later have to come
to terms with what you believe. Not with what a church says you
should believe or what a creed says somebody else believed but with
what you actually do believe. Start there. It may not be much, but
it's honest. What's the gain, anyway, of saying you believe something if you don't? Or of trying to believe something if you don't?
Whom are you fooling? Not God certainly!

Every period of history has its own characterizing word which,
more aptly than any other, expresses the mood of the time. Long-
fellow had what was perhaps the word for his era when he wrote
of "A banner with the strange device, Excelsior!" meaning, "ever

higher!" That has been the keynote of a good many periods of history, and it is even now not altogether obsolete. *Patience* has been the keynote of some others, *action* of others, *believing* of yet others.

Today's banner, it is embarrassingly clear, bears the word *unbelievingness*. We're all so conscious of this that we've given it a name: the credibility gap. These days you can hardly say anything about anything or hear anything about anything without taking the credibility gap—your own or someone else's—into account. We're just not of a mood to accept anything at face value. We've been gulled, sweet-talked, sour-talked, manipulated, managed, talked down to and —we might as well be realistic about it—lied to, until we have little capacity left for believing.

Our own emotional avarice has contributed. We've got into the habit of expecting a percentage to be knocked off the list price—of everything. Then in order for it to be knocked off, the list price was raised—a phony base for a phony discount. That makes everybody, the theory goes, equally happy. The theory could just as well go that it makes everybody equally unhappy. So many transactions have been reduced to exercises in bargaining, neither party believing a word the other says and striking a deal only after there has been haggling-down from too much on one side and haggling-up from too little on the other. This may be a great way for a Cairo bazaar to do business, but it would sure slow things down in a supermarket.

Anyway, there's no sale—of goods or ideas—until the credibility gap is eliminated.

Take government in this country, for one example. Washington was the birthplace of the credibility gap; it was to describe what was happening there, or what people thought was happening, that somebody thought up the name. People have had the feeling repeatedly that the government was not leveling with them, that it regarded people as only incidental to the show it ran—a kind of avoidable nuisance. To say this doesn't prove that you are a Republican or a a Democrat, only that you can read.

In Washington, the creeping escalation of the Vietnam war contributed massively to the credibility gap. It was supposed to be quick and easy. Only a few advisers. Then a few thousand. Then 400,000 troops and who knows how long? Part of the difficulty is the fact that the government is not omniscient and has to change its mind like us ordinary mortals. But to admit this is apparently against the rules, and to deny it gives rise to the reasonable accusation that the government doesn't think our nerves are as good as its own. Government too often has cried "Sheep!"

In political and international relations, do we always *have* to think we're getting a world-beating bargain and the other fellow was taken to the cleaners? Isn't there any satisfaction any longer in just getting something for something?

The trouble with credibility gaps, in government and out, is that the next one is always wider than the last one. It's infectious. It takes a heap of truth-telling to expunge an incredible government cover-up from the subconscious. In a socialist society, this probably doesn't matter. In a free, self-governing society, it matters very much. I must be able to believe my government and it simply must trust me, if its capabilities and therefore my own are not to be destroyed. Just give me the facts—don't confuse me by trying to make up my mind.

The credibility gap is at one of its most visible levels in religion. This is what the new, radical theologies, the threatened heresy trials, the Vatican Council, the ecumenical movement, the jolts and surprises are all about. These are all a part of the rebellion against the credibility gap. You hear people saying that Christianity must be relevant—another way of saying that it must be believable here and now. A lot of doctrines are, to put it inelegantly, in drydock for a hull-scraping job, a clearing away of clinging barnacles that over the years have attached themselves, obscuring what's underneath. And as anyone who has ever had anything to do with them knows, barnacles give the scraper no cooperation whatsoever.

The trouble with so many aspects of what we defensively and inexactly call "faith" is that they have about the same credibility level as television commercials—it never occurs to the viewer that he is expected to *believe* them! It's a sort of game that everybody plays—the sponsor feeling that he doesn't have to make sense, only noise, and the viewers that now is the time to duck out to the refrigerator for a quick snack. This is not to say that there is not a certain subliminal level of belief in either living room or pew, only that it is of a different order of importance from believing that you have to get up when the alarm clock rings tomorrow morning.

The religious credibility gap feeds on all sorts of things. For one, on our preoccupation with the packaging of theological concepts. That is, one presumes there are concepts in those packages. There were once, anyway. But when somebody got them all nicely wrapped and sealed in church councils and creeds and prayer books and what not, it seemed not only a shame to open them up for a look, but almost sacrilegious. Meanwhile, the wrappings grew soiled and yellowed—and hallowed. The big stir going on now is that the boxes are being opened and rewrapped—and you would think it was the end of the world (or that these new wrappings were going to last forever)!

For another thing, we've tried from the pew to "manage" the pulpit, and from the pulpit to "manage" the pew. We've been afraid to let ideas stand or fall in the open market. Not all the thumbs on scales in this world have been in butcher shops; a lot of them have been in churches. If a congregation is afraid to let its minister level with them, or if the minister thinks his version of truth is too potent and that he'd better not "alienate" his people, a credibility gap is piling up somewhere, and when it lets go there will be more alienation than you can shake a vestment at.

The church is the one you hear crying "Wolf!" And though there have been some fairly significant wolves onstage in history from time to time, the ultimate, cataclysmic, Armageddon-sized wolf just hasn't come off. Matter of fact, you can detect some signs of improvement in the world once in a while. Not even the threat of atomic holocaust has kept very many people awake very many nights, as far as I can tell, and I guess we're supposed to feel guilty about that. Wolf is not selling any better than sheep these days. Especially in church.

One could go on listing credibility-gap manifestations. Take the John F. Kennedy assassination theories. On that one, the public wouldn't believe a deposition from the angel Gabriel at this point. Mention flying saucers. Or fluoridation. Or anything. Man, we're skeptical about everything! And that's a real sickness.

Strong medicine is required, and I think I know what it is: *Truth*. That's one of the miracle drugs, you know. There may be side effects, but we must take desperate measures. Let's give it straight, take it straight. We're adults, we Americans, we Christians. Aren't we? We don't have to be babied, shielded, cued in on when to grin, when to shiver. Do we? Personally, I don't want to be told only what somebody, with the best or the worst of intentions, thinks I *ought* to know.

Truth can't be manipulated anyway—not for very long. Not by press agentry, not by injunction. Not by pew or pulpit or White House or your house or mine.

20) What in the world is it all about?

The antics of some believers not only make believing hard for some of us—we do our worst to make it hard for ourselves. For we do our believing in words, not in ideas. Many of the words are inadequate. It's as if we were sick and went to the doctor and he gave us a prescription and we chewed up and swallowed down the prescription blank. What he scribbled and handed us has to be translated into a pill, a capsule, a liquid. The "translation" process is the one we often leave out of our faith. We gulp down whatever somebody hands us without trying to find out first, "What does it mean?" We do this very often from force of habit—"streptomycin" or "salvation" or "born again" are such reassuring words—or because we are satisfied with a faith off the rack instead of custom-made, or because making our own decisions is just too confusing.

If, for example, you were to ask me why our family sits in the balcony at our church, I would have to go back almost twenty years and practically into my subconscious to come up with the answer.

When we first moved to town, we intended to visit several churches before deciding where we wished to cast our lot, but we never got farther than the first one. We decided this was where we wanted to be, and here we have been ever since.

Our younger daughter was nursery-sized, and the nursery was located on the second floor, off the corridor behind the sanctuary balcony. Sometimes she required consoling, and so her mother and I found that if we sat in the balcony, we—or more especially she— would be easily available. Then two sons came along and the arrangement continued.

Now the children are children no more. Even the church structure is no more—parts of it were demolished and parts incorporated into the construction of a modern office building that houses, among other enterprises, an insurance company and a language school. The congregation built a new church home in another section of town where week-night parking was less exasperating. The new church also had a balcony, and automatically our family staked out a pew there, though there was no nursery adjacent and we had no need for one.

For us, the balcony lost its utilitarianism but became a habit. When we sit on the ground level to accommodate visiting friends and relatives who do not take kindly to stair-climbing, I feel vaguely uncomfortable and somehow out of it.

I do not think I am any more set in my ways than the next person, and indeed I regard myself as a rather red-blooded, soft-arteried, adaptable citizen. Maybe it's just that we each have our own special thing which inadvertently demonstrates how easy it is to confuse means with ends, highways with destinations. We lose sight of what things and ideas are all about. The "aboutness" gets swept away, forgotten, sometimes outlived. And years, decades, centuries later we find ourselves earnestly contending for the need to be in one balcony or another, when there is no need at all. It would have quite a calming influence if we would once in a while back off and ask, "Why am I here?"

Try it on religion. We get so involved in *expressions* of ideas in creeds, dogmas, doctrines, even Bible stories or statements that we forget the ideas themselves. The expression of a truth is not that truth itself. Whether found in a creed or a text it is a kind of "He went that way" pointer. But how absorbed we become with the pointers. How readily we mobilize at some crossroads to fight, bleed, and die, not for the Holy City but for the signpost that points the way to it! Instead of pondering what it is that holy or human writ is trying to tell us, we get hung up on the telling. "The form of godliness" gets priority over the power of godliness, the expression over that which is expressed. We've become in so many ways worshipers of words.

Take some of the classic examples. Even to comment on the doctrine we have come to call the Virgin Birth is to set off a Distant Early Warning alert. Klaxons blare, outposts scramble, planes take to the air just in case the comment turns out to be hostile. Not until intruders have spoken the proper code words are the fighters called in and does the base return to normal. Yet the doctrine of the Virgin Birth is surely not an end in itself. It is a way of saying something vitally important about God's relationship to man, his identification with the human predicament, his love for the world, his caring. We've taken that tremendously significant reality and tried to make a medical case history of it. We dare to ask God, "Where were you on the night of March 25?" We try to imprison him within our own small minds and comprehensions. But God will not be imprisoned. He evades us down the corridors of time, eludes all that we can say about him. To assume that God must do things the way we think he should have done or do them, and that he must explain his actions to our complete satisfaction, is to miss the point. God is not on the witness stand, and we are attorneys neither for the defense nor for the prosecution.

On other doctrines—attempts, all, to describe the mighty acts of God—our ignition thresholds are only a little higher. The Second Coming, to name one. When I was seventeen or so, I could have told you exactly what was coming next, world with end. I listened avidly to Bible teachers who had the future all lined out on the authority of the books of Daniel and Revelation. It may be that all they taught will indeed someday come to pass, though it is difficult to run a check on these things. But is that what eschatology (the study of last things) is all about? Were the visions written to give us a schedule for what will happen the first hour after we die or the world dies and what will then happen after that, or are they saying something much more ultimate? Are they not rather saying that God will somehow, in his own way and in his own time, have the last word? That we can never outrun God's compulsive, relentless love? That there is no place to hide? That somewhere, somehow, we shall have to confront Truth and that this moment of truth—or eon of truth—will reveal us to ourselves? Punishment, reward, who rules what and where and for how many millennia—these are not the prior questions. If we believe the promise, "Where I am, there shall you be also," who needs a timetable?

The Lord's Supper, the Christian's dramatic demonstration of unity, has walled Christian brother from brother for scores of generations and continues to do so. Unity has become picayunity. Individual glasses or a common cup? How often? Who? How? Stay in the pew or go to the altar rail? Even the question of whether the elements become actual flesh and blood or merely symbolize the Lord's body seems unimportant (and in no way changes the facts, in any case) in view of the "aboutness" of the ordinance (or sacrament): our need to identify ourselves with the Lord, in truth to "commune" with him and to do it together. This is a family-style meal, for this is the Christian family. We have made it into a spiritual drive-in where we never get out of our shells, never relate to the rest of the family and particularly not to our religious in-laws.

One could go on, and I intend to do just that in my own thinking and I hope that you will do it in yours. The key word, it seems to me—the word that unites us, the word that cools our misdirected passions, the word that keeps calling us back to priorities—is "aboutness." *What is it all about?* Answer that, and the chances are you're immediately a little less steamy and stuffy in all kinds of contexts.

What is a job all about? Lose sight of this and all you wind up with is a paycheck, which, despite its usefulness, can never be big enough to buy a man's life.

What is law and order all about? If what we're looking for are people who are willing to starve in an orderly manner, forget it. If what we're looking for are people content to be lawfully ignored or harassed or satisfied with the leavings we grandly push under the table, we're going to be—providentially—disappointed. Law and order are the means toward the health of the body politic, toward, as we like to put it, "the pursuit of happiness." But the fun of pursuit wears off unless you catch something once in a while. If there's no end to support the means, or even if numbers of people are convinced there is not, then they will find new means. This, men have done from time immemorial, and it should be no great surprise to anyone.

What is America all about? Those leaders who have had visions and have dreamed dreams have been the ones who made us greater than we were, though some of them lost their lives in the process. There has been something of the poet in them—the ability to see far and to encourage us to stand on tiptoe to see it, too. We in America have a way of killing our statesmen, poets, and prophets who try to tell us that America is not about self-seeking and money-making and taxes and the latest model of everything and crabgrass-free lawns. It is about—and this is the hope of all faith—a shining idea, a challenging ideal that someday we may reach if we do not altogether forget where to look.

Clichés—religious and otherwise—are the opiate of the people.

21) Lapel-button theology

In New York, the lapel-button fad quickly escalated uptown from Greenwich Village. "God Is Alive and Well in Mexico City." "Join the Pope's Rhythm Band." "Is There Life after Birth?" Buttons like that. Some of them satirical. Some of them irreverent. Some sharp. Some dull. Some outrageous. Some worse than that.

These things go in cycles. Buttons of an earlier era expressed such philosophical comments as "I Love My Wife, but Oh You Kid!" And about the turn of the century, leather postcards, of all things, were mailed with boldness and received with blushes and sometimes were stitched together into sofa pillows. When I was a boy, exploring one rainy afternoon in a family trunk (whatever became of trunks?), I came upon a bundle of leather postcards my father had sent my mother during their courting days. The racy sentiment on one read, "My only books were women's looks, and follies all they taught me." For well over forty years those lines have stuck in my mind, which probably would prove something to a psychiatrist.

The button bent—saying something short and snappy—has been with us a long time, and has been often a political device. In 1844, some Americans were crying, "54-40 or Fight!" It had to do with the Oregon question and war with England. The numbers referred to 54° 40′ north latitude, a line on the map. The slogan would have looked good on a button, if they had had buttons then, and it was easy to say and to get excited about. But President Polk settled for the 49th parallel without fighting and a lot of people had to turn in their slogan. At the end of Woodrow Wilson's first term, button-talk said, "He Kept Us Out of War." During his next term, he didn't, and couldn't, and We Made the World Safe for Democracy.

At one time or another we have had the Big Stick and the Square Deal and the New Deal and the Big Deal. Britain had her Finest Hour, we remembered Pearl Harbor, we got this nation moving again, we explored the New Frontier and set up the Great Society, and made things perfectly clear. In betweentimes, we worked for a Just and Durable Peace, invented the Free World and developed an Alliance for Progress. It was and is and ever shall be, government by epigram. Make it short, make it simple, solve the world's ills with the turn of a phrase.

But the world is complicated, fearfully and wonderfully inter-related. Our parts are like the planets wheeling in space, every one reacting to every other. One of them couldn't be plucked out of position unless the rest were all rearranged. Some clear night, take a look into the sky and ponder the stupendous juggling act. In microcosm, the same thing is happening in this one little world where we live, and in micro-microcosm, in any city neighborhood where dozens of

obscure shops stay solvent because they draw customers from somewhere, meanwhile giving their business somewhere else. Government
by epigram deals with one small piece of the world, one community
of interest at a time, as if everything else will politely stand still
while we tinker with Cuba or the Middle East or Indochina or whatever. What we do in any of those places affects what is happening
everywhere else. The armaments industry, for example, shudders at
the thought of peace—and you can see it shudder on a stock ticker.
It is a sobering and terrible thing to develop a vested interest in chaos
—and before any of us throws a first stone, let us ponder where our
own dividends are coming from.

Nothing is as simple—about anything—as the button boys would
like to charm us into thinking. "Impeach Spiro Agnew!"—and then
what? "Kill a Commie for Christ"—and then what? Whom do you
impeach or kill next? When is the job done, and what job?

There are ideas and movements and currents that are simply too
big, too complex to put on buttons. "Forget Pearl Harbor" doesn't
say it any better than "Remember Pearl Harbor." There are things
about it to be remembered and things to be forgotten, and you can't
get that into either jingoistic, smug little slogan. Substitute "Hiro-
shima" for "Pearl Harbor" and the same is true. Perhaps the only
deliverance we can expect lies in recognizing, by hindsight generally,
our inadequacies as human beings at any given moment of crisis,
rather than in retroactive whitewashing or blackwashing. Life is
infinitely complex and human reactions are vulnerable and fallible
always, and you can't say all that on a button.

It's problem enough when button-thinking obscures or dominates
political thinking, but it is even more of a problem when this is
true of religious thinking. Theology by epigram is, unfortunately,
not just this year's religious fad. It is the historic way of measuring
commitment, whether one's own or that of others. We want it quick
and we want it simple and we want it certain sure, and perhaps it
cannot be any of these.

In one traditional manifestation, the button reads, "Are You
Saved?" The expected answer has been "Yes" or "No," but it could

as well be, "From what?" For there is a great deal of theology wrapped up in both the question and in any answer, and I'm not sure that we can be as cryptic as all that except with those who have cracked the code. But, usually, as long as the person asking the question gets a Yes answer, however fast, slow, embarrassed or puzzled, that may be all he wants. He can then go on his way satisfied that he has done his stint of "witnessing" for the day. It's as if the Good Samaritan had said to the fellow lying in the ditch, "Are you alive?" and gone happily down the road when he heard a groan. There are some things you can never get on a button, and for some reason it's awfully hard to make some people understand this.

In religion there are as many buttons as there are doctrines. Every denomination has its own buttons. Every band of the conservative-liberal spectrum has its own buttons. Every faith has its own.

If you sport a particular button, or let somebody pin it on you, you're accepted by whoever is purveying that button. If you don't, you're not. But is it that simple? It's like a lawyer fixing a stern gaze on the witness and demanding, "Where were you on the night of May 24? Answer Yes or No." There are some questions that you just can't answer Yes or No—either because such an answer is not relevant at all or because it's not clear what the question is.

I have the sneaking suspicion that a lot of this bent toward dogmatic buttonism is not the result of Christian zeal at all, but of Christian unconcern. We're not enough interested in people to care what they mean when they reply, or what they think we mean when we ask the question. To put it another way, we seem to be more interested in answers than we are in answerers.

Perhaps the most untouchable sacrament in the church is Conformation. To require a person to conform to what we think he should be doesn't require too much of him—only that he give up his personhood. The bind in which the church finds itself increasingly is that more and more people are deciding that this is too high a price.

For some folk, religious button-thinking is not a problem, and blessings on them. Probably for all of us, *some* buttons are not a problem. In our own minds, we make an automatic adjustment, take in the idea here, let it out there, so that it fits what we truly believe. But what about the man or woman or young person who comes cold to a mode of expressing ideas as big as God is big. Must his words in his situation be the same as my words in mine? Will I be ill-at-ease until he pins on my approved button? Does, indeed, truth always have to be tidily packaged? Must it be reduced to words that will fit on a button or in a creed?

True, you're advised to be ready to "give a reason for the faith that is within you." But nobody said it has to be in five snappy words.

Or in one infallibly detailed set of instructions, for that matter.

22) "You go south to the Equator and turn left"

That was the answer I received from a friend who had served as a missionary in Africa, when I asked him where his country was located. His fun-loving reply made at least as much sense as the old geography-book way of saying, "bounded on the north by the Federation of Mombasa and on the south by Eastern Equatorial Bechuanaland" or something like that, for by the time anybody had grown up enough to go, the countries had new names. This kind of thing is disconcerting to me, for I'm a compulsive sign-reader. Furthermore, I tend to do what the signs say, and even to take some small satisfaction in it.

For example, I get my kicks out of streaking past a radar unit in a fifty-mile-an-hour zone at fifty miles an hour. Though I must admit I grew impatient one recent pre-dawn morning when on otherwise vacant city streets I was detained by one mindless stoplight after another until each whimsically turned green. I kept telling myself that I was adding stamina to my reflexes, in whose hands my motoring life so often rests. The trouble was that other reflexes kept insisting, "But no other car is in sight!" In such circumstances, one's disenchantment with irrational, automated law wipes out the satisfaction of being sign-abiding.

My serious quarrel is with signs that are ambiguous, or worse. For years, my wife and I went into shock every time we drove south on Route 1, bound for the Massachusetts Turnpike, and approached the much-clover-leafed intersection with Route 128, which circles around Boston. Route 128 is the greatest blow for freedom since the patriots made their stand at Lexington and Concord, and delivers the motorist from the hapless fate of finding his way through downtown Boston. But year after year, I was at the last minute unclear about which way to turn. I wanted to go west, but all I was offered was SOUTH SHORE, which sounded to me like east, and BEVERLY, which I haven't located yet. Either we made the wrong turn, Labor Day after Labor Day, thinking it was the right turn, or we made the right turn with the dark suspicion that it was the wrong one.

Then, one year, "our" interchange was newly labeled MASSACHU-SETTS TURNPIKE and even as a kindly afterthought, NEW YORK. Obviously, we hadn't been the only ones who had turned toward (or was it away from?) Beverly. Signs, I am beginning to realize, are made by people who already know where they are, and who can't quite convince themselves that anyone could or should wish to go farther.

But that is just one small aspect of my personal crusade for clear labeling. Another concerns the penchant of some sign-placers for getting you started off on some road and then suddenly deserting you down the line somewhere. It happened to us at North Windham, Maine. A sign at an intersection pointed invitingly to what sounded like an interesting antique shop, and we turned in that direction. A hundred yards along, another sign carefully steered us onto a dirt road. Now we were hooked, and the sign-people knew it. When we came to a fork in the road they had lost interest: no sign. Choosing the more likely branch, we bumped on, and on, eventually to turn back and voice a few choice thoughts about people whose signs abandon you in the middle of nowhere.

Other signs promise more than you find when you get there, a case of oversnow. Others are like the gems we found near Biddeford. A roadside shop had a big OPEN sign in front. We were into the parking area before we saw the CLOSED sign in the window. It became perfectly clear: he was open for the season but closed for the day. Inscrutable signmanship!

The crushing example occurred just two or three counties from home. On a little-traveled highway, we became aware that the gasoline gauge needle was near bottom. Fortuitously, we came upon a gas station with our brand of credit card. Heaving a sign of relief, I pulled up alongside a pump. An attendant came over and said with some embarrassment, "We're out of gas."

Forgotten signs that direct you to places that are no longer there, that promise more than they can possibly deliver, that are ambiguous or incomplete are one side of all this. The other is the oral signboard, the person who tells you how to get somewhere. It has been my experience that you have to be especially wary of the fellow who says cheerfully, 'You can't miss it!" Maybe *he* couldn't miss it, but I could. He has the same handicap that the sign-planters have—he's on home territory. Familiarity breeds, among other things, unintelligibility. In one sense, you may get better directions from the man who has never been there, though I am not quite certain for what sermon that is a proper text.

But without question, the signboard mystique has implications for religious faith. I am beginning to feel that I and a lot of other people have expected a great deal more in the way of explicit directions from the church than we had any right to expect or than it had any right to promise. Though most of the guilt has been in our own excessive assumptions, there has been ecclesiastical oversnow, too. The church has had a great deal to say about the road to peace, but we never arrived. And about the misuse of money and pride and comfort and others of the daintier sins. Corporately, we the church have promised more than we have delivered. The signs said it would be easy to be the kind of Christian we had in mind, and it turned out to be not only difficult but impossible.

On the other hand, we direction-seekers asked for too much. We wanted the signs to say, TURN LEFT HERE and we would turn, and TURN RIGHT HERE and we would turn, and GO SLOW and we would go slowly, and STOP and we would stop. What we wanted was a super-highway to the Kingdom with all the directions in the new white-on-green, larged-sized luminous lettering, and a seventy-mile speed limit. We wanted it so that there would be no possibility of getting off course, no chance of being stranded somewhere.

What we got was an imperfectly marked road that didn't even show on the map! Some of us felt cheated. The signs were confusing. We didn't know for sure which way to go. And sometimes, when we went the way a sign pointed, nothing was there.

We wanted to make sure the church had a steeple that pointed "heavenward" and was uncompromised by any "fickle" weather-vane symbolism that pointed now here, now there, as the wind blew. Then we realized—painfully realized—that God was no more up than he was down and that the weather vane, pointing us every which way, showed us where God and our responsibility really were —not up, but here, there, everywhere.

The signs for the faithful are just not as precise as we once thought they were, and this is quite an admission for an old sign-crusader like myself. We can't even assume that the gas station will always have gas. There might be some useful humility in the church's occasional admission that it, too, has to get its fuel from a bigger bulk tank.

There are no indisputably visible, large-sized markings, I am convinced, that will take us through life allowing us total certainty at every turn that we are on the right track. I was about to say it would be nice if there were. Well, maybe it would be nice, but it wouldn't be faith. For faith, as we so easily forget, is the evidence of things *not* seen. Faith is the daring that leads you down an unmarked road and never lets you be 100 per cent certain-sure that it is the Way.

They had their spiritual superhighways in biblical times, come to think of it, as we have them literally and figuratively today. The Bible calls it the "broad way," but says it leads to destruction. The road that gets to where I assume we want to go is narrow, not much traveled, unimproved, unnumbered—the worst kind of road for signs. You'll probably have to stop many times and ask for directions.

If you do and some optimist tells you, "Full speed ahead, you can't miss it!" you're lost, man. But if somebody else delays you with a tale of woe, presses you into service, hates to see you go, take heart. It could be the right road after all. For being a Christian means, in some very special sense, being needed and wanted. It doesn't mean getting home free, but sharing yourself as you go.

23) It doesn't say, "Ye are the potatoes of the earth"

It wouldn't say potatoes anyway, since this is not one of the cash crops of the land whose flora and fauna provided the metaphors and parables of Scripture. Perhaps wheat or barley would do, but since my cooking prowess is limited to heating a TV dinner, and I'm not sure what salt has to do with wheat or barley, and this is going to be about salt, I will, with all due respect to biblical scholarship, stick to potatoes. In my part of the world, anybody can recognize a potato when he sees one, and most of us can recognize one when we taste it, fried, baked, boiled, or mashed. A western Christian can identify with a potato. And in any of its culinary incarnations, a potato—for most people—needs salt.

The point of all this is that we usually act as if we had been commissioned to be potatoes, rather than to be salt. "Ye are the *salt* of the earth," Jesus told his disciples. Salt is supposed to do something to something else. If we can get hold of that ordinary, little-obvious fact about salt, it makes life a lot more fun and a lot less burdensome.

For then, you don't have to be everything and do everything. All you have to do is salt it down.

The trouble is that this is not as easy as it looks. To do it, you have to admit to the integrity of other people and even of other people than Christians. You have to admit that other groups than the church are doing good, valid things, and that just because what they're doing didn't get started in the glow of a stained-glass window doesn't mean that it is without merit and that the church has to set up a counterpart movement with the name Christian attached to sanctify it. The task of the Christian is to supply salt, meaning, flavor, zest. Yet we've all been running around, spreading ourselves thin, wearing ourselves out, trying to be potatoes. Not only were we not good at the masquerade, but we were wasting our mission. We became clannish. We found our own kind and set up housekeeping. If there was an organization for lawyers, for example, we weren't content until we had set up an organization for Christian lawyers. We wanted either to manage everything or to ignore it, and nobody much had enough courage or enough confidence in his seasoning ability to be what every Christian is declared by his nature to be: salt.

Actually, what is salt good for, except to be expended, used up, on something other than itself? Salt, no matter how potent its savor, is no good by itself. You can't eat it. And who wants salt-on-salt? But it's the rare person—and the rare Christian—who appears to be willing to spend himself to enhance the flavor of something or somebody else.

I often think of a secret that Lillian Dickson has lived and worked by in her amazing Formosan ministry: "You can do anything in this world that you want to do and that needs doing, if you don't care who gets the credit for it." That is the way salt works. I've never heard anybody say, upon forking in a mouthful of mashed potatoes, "My, but this salt tastes good!" Yet that's the kind of comment we who are supposed to be the salt of the earth seem to be doing our best to elicit about ourselves.

There is this about salt that should make us think twice before fishing for compliments or even expecting them: The only time you can taste salt is when you've got too much of it in something. The analogies here for church people are pointed and numerous: we've all known somebody like that, who's been too self-promoting, and the chances are that we've all been somebody like that. The analogies for the church at large are also uncomfortable ones: the church may be least sacrificial, least the servant church, when it is being most visible. The church may be doing worst what it is supposed to be doing—salting—when it is trying hardest to be the whole show.

A cold, sober fact of life is that it takes a lot more potatoes than salt to run the world. A little salt can go a long way. Ounce for ounce, pound for pound, the impact of salt has it all over the impact of potatoes. But to make the impact, the salt must get in touch with the potatoes. Christians have been so afraid of dirtying their hands or their minds or their dogmas that they've avoided "the world" like the plague. Yet, that's where the salting has to be done.

What, I wonder, are we saving our salt for? Is it just that the right stew hasn't come along? In the meantime, the world has managed surprisingly well on what we would like to presume is a salt-free diet. Could it be that someone else will be, and has been, the salt of the earth, if we won't be? Salt has been sought for and fought for through history. People have been determined to have it—food would be a tasteless disaster without it. Life also would be, and is, a chronic case of the blahs without "salt." People are determined to have it—if not from one source, then from another; if not from Christians, then from wherever some kind of seasoning, however phony it seems to us, can be had.

What would happen if we let ourselves go? If we let our faith out of the shaker? If we stopped attacking the motives and methods of everybody else in the world, and added what it is we can add—zest, confidence, purposefulness, love, compassion? What would happen if we tried giving ourselves away? Suppose we were to make a determined effort to understand someone with whom we disagree, to try putting ourselves in his frame of reference, see what the view is from there? What if we tried a daring application of love in a situation that has gone sour, said to ourselves, "What is the most

loving response I can make to it *right now?*"—and made it? What
if we took personal inventory this minute, singled out someone
within our daily orbit we do not really care about, deliberately
decided to care? What if we said, "How can I, by what I do today,
improve the flavor of life in my home, my church, my community,
my country?"—and did it? What if we said, "Now, just once in
my life, I will risk even my beliefs for what I believe—as I so
regularly and fearlessly risk my money for the prospect of gain, or
my life for the prospect of happiness"? What if our rationale for
daring were not always, "But that's business!" and were sometimes,
"But that's faith!"

In short, what if we got out of the potato business, where we
don't belong, and into the salt business, where we do belong?

Salt is that extra something, that plus, that life-style, which should
be the distinguishing mark of the Christian as he moves among people. It is what he possesses to give, not what he possesses to keep.
It is not cumbersome, heavy-handed, but lissome, winsome, joyous.
To the place where he is, the Christian adds a hope; an outlook, an
excitement that it would not have without him. He does not supplant
what is, but wakes it, bring out the best in it, nudges it more alive,
more noble than it knew it was or could be. Salt brings out the
hidden capacity of men to be the children of God. And we instead
have tried to intimidate them into the Kingdom, preach them in
from a riskless distance, argue them in, scare them in, entice them
in, all the while withholding ourselves.

It will be a small world and a small Kingdom if we can enjoy
only that piece of it created or re-created in our own image. It will
be an immense task if we have to build every stick and stone of it
from scratch. No wonder we feel overwhelmed! Our job is to season
what is already there, sharing the qualities that are our calling.

To do that, we have to know what is already there—and something more.

24) Telling it like it could be

"Tell it like it is" is a great credo. And it's not new. Every once in a while an old idea falls into disrepair and somebody has to rediscover it and put it into words that are freshly abrasive enough to cut through our comfortable adjustment to old words. That's what happened with this admonition. Jesus, of course, was one of the all-time experts at telling it like it was, and still is.

For general purposes, the credo is a handy one to have around the house, be it house of worship, White House, your house, my house. Many times during this or any year we will have need to invoke its humbling and even humiliating dynamic—in personal life, business life, national life, religious life. But for many, hearing it told like it is will be a fate worse than death.

For at least three reasons we are prone to become card-carrying citizens of the psychological State of Euphoria. Some of us are, in one niche or another of our reactions, lazy, let's face it. There is simply no gentler word for it. Facing facts is just too wearying. Today, anyway. Maybe next week, next year. But unfaced facts have a way, sooner or later, of backing us into corners, and when the inescapable moment of truth arrives, the chances are we will be a good deal wearier than we are now. Besides, the nearer to a corner one is pushed, the fewer are the options that remain open.

There are some who believe automatically and even as an article of faith and/or patriotism that all is well, and if they should hear glimmerings that it isn't, their normal response is to clobber the glimmerers. This is one of the standard reactions of all times up to and including the future. The problem itself is seldom as reachable as the person who says there is a problem. Thus, the naïve assumption has arisen (and continues to arise) that if you can just eliminate *him* you have dealt adequately with *it*. The arsenal of elimination contains all kinds of weapons from livelihood-taking to life-taking. We get more easily upset about who's bugging us than about what's bugging him.

Then, there are some who suspect that all may be considerably unwell, but who because of a vested interest are not about to publicize their suspicions. They sense that under the frantic façade of activity there is a used-up emptiness. But you don't raise money by brashly announcing that the faith of our fathers' sons is a floodlighted sepulcher full of dead men's bones. These people wish they could make things right before they admit that anything is wrong which needs righting—a philosophy that makes for a certain amount of confusion, like a family moving into an apartment which the previous tenants have not yet vacated.

Whether it's lazy ignorance or devout ignorance or selfish ignorance, it reacts badly to tellers-like-it-is—one of the most easily demonstrable facts of life, in or out of Scripture. So, true to form, most of us will work religiously at maintaining the shouts of triumphalism, respecting the evidence that supports our position, rejecting the rest. In church, we will go on singing hymns of victory— or more often, paying somebody to sing them for us. We will, when the order of worship indicates, thank God from whom all blessings flow. We will have the usual things to say about peace on earth, but we will be careful not to let our espousal of peace interfere with "real life," which includes war. We will listen to the story of the Good Samaritan, piously hope we are he and not the priest or Levite, never for a moment consider that what we really may be is one of the thieves the victim fell among.

We need tellers-like-it-is, for the bread of life, fresh from the oven, grows stale, then shrivels, finally petrifies. Without quite realizing what has happened, we feed stones to our children and grow sluggish ourselves with their weight.

Refusal to face up to reality offers bliss, but only for a while.

Now and then we need to see and be seen with stark honesty. From even a hamburger stand we require a once-a-year balance sheet, audited and certified. From a Christian or a faith or a nationalism, we don't require much of anything. Yet, telling it like it is, jarring as this may be at times, is our salvation. Far from being quick to stifle honesty, we ought to swallow our pride and encourage it. Dissent should be heard and not seen. If dissent were heard, maybe it wouldn't have to be seen.

But where do we go from here? What lies beyond what is? We act as if telling it like it is constitutes the only reality, and forget that when we've got telling, immediately therewith we've got viewpoint, interpretation, bias. "Reality" is not a very helpful word, either, for what is real and what isn't? Is reality the worst, and nothing better, that life has to offer?

That is what one would think. For what happens, it seems to me, when we go overboard on the "as is" side, is that we easily become mired down. (Just as, on the other side, we tend to float meaninglessly in space.) A little mire is good for the soul. But who wants to bog down there? Apparently some people do—and for what they, too, believe are religious reasons. One can become so enamored of, so intrigued with, so shocked by the discovery of personal, religious, or national emptiness that one thinks it offers a lifelong career and decides to settle in.

I get the feeling that this has happened to, among others, the motion picture industry. A few years back, film producers listened to somebody who said, "Tell it like it is!" and they never got over it. They discovered all kinds of things that most of us didn't know about, and they made movies out of them. To read the pages advertising today's motion pictures, you would think that lust, violence, brutality, and general kook-ism prevail.

What happens to some of the characters in the movies today shouldn't happen to a dog—and doesn't. We're going to have to find a more accurate way of talking about "animal passions" or "barnyard morals." Such epithets insult the animals. The average barnyard is a study in propriety, compared with the motion picture pages of the *New York Times*.

Specialists who are versed in animal husbandry may know of a prurient pig or two or a perverted Leghorn, but I doubt if it's very common. Only man has the capacity to act like something he is not. And we've been getting long looks at him in his worst moments. Not only in the movies, either, but on the stage, in books—and in pulpits. It's all brushed off with the wide-eyed apology, "But that's the way it is, man!"

That's the way *what* is? Sure, you can find this sort of thing, and a lot more they haven't even discovered yet. But that's not the way it *all* is. Telling it like it is, is supposed to provide some impetus to move into what it could be. The Prodigal Son lived in his own kind of dream world—thinking he could live forever on his father's capital. He couldn't, and when his resources ran out, his friends began telling it like it was. He wound up feeding hogs. Color that "realism". Then this interesting sentence, "When he came to himself. . . ." When that happened, he cut out and hurried home. Color *that* "realism," too! The one thing the account doesn't say is that he never forgot what he had seen, he never forgot the rumbles of his empty stomach. I would guess, too, that despite religious convictions, he had a lifelong affection for pigs, for in their company, "he came to himself."

Have we come to ourselves?

There's surely a better world out there somewhere. This is not only the American Dream, but the Christian hope. This has been the motivation of every scientist, every explorer, every social worker, every minister, every parent. Let's see where we are—certainly! But when we find out, we don't have to stay there. There comes a time when we must say, if we are to be men, "This is not where I want to be. My destiny is ahead, and I'm moving out to meet it!"

25) Who shall roll us away
the stone?

There is one destiny for which we use all sorts of evasive words to avoid the need of calling it what it is—death. We like to think that we know so much about it, but honesty insists that we know so little. Is it a journey of no return? Is it a journey to continuing existence? If so, what kind of existence? Where shall we live? How? On what plane of consciousness? The barrage of question marks surrounding this second most determinative event in life (birth—or conception—being the other) makes it either a fear-filled or a faith-satisfied contemplation.

The line between concern, which is good, and worry, which is not, lies somewhere in a vaguely defined and perhaps undefinable everyman's land. Yet, depending upon the placing of that line, careers are built or eroded, sanity is maintained or shattered, life is lived confidently or fearfully. Curiosity, we tell inquisitive children, killed the cat, and yet the child—or even the cat—who has no curiosity at all is not equipped to cope with his own existence. Every sermonizer who has expounded upon the "take no thought for the morrow" theme has, we dare say, had to squeeze in edgewise a defense of the desirability of *some* thought-taking—canned goods in the pantry, ground round steak in the freezer, money in the bank, a life insurance policy (how do you *insure* a life?) in force.

To shingle the roof for a rainy day is regarded as more orthodox than unorthodox, despite the Sermon on the Mount. (Preachers solve the problem by saying it doesn't mean *that*.) At the same time, everyone knows that it is quite altogether possible to acquire a shingle- or a freezer- or a fiscal-fixation that results in a paralyzing preoccupation with tomorrow. (And without doubt the Sermon on the Mount does mean *this*.)

Though no insurance agent will happily tolerate the expression "insurance poor," perhaps even they will accept the validity of the theological concept of the same name. That concept goes like this: in our much squirreling away of things and assurances, we are prone to forget that there is a today and that it has a very high priority in the scheme of things. As of this moment, we are not dwelling in Beulah Land.

The trouble with us is that we want to have our today and our tomorrow too. We want the mystery demystified, the yearning reduced to a mathematical equation, hope programed for a computer, things-seen to be the evidence of faith. We want everything worked out for us ahead of time and we want to know precisely how it is to be worked out and when and where and why.

Perhaps this is a peculiarly American trait. When it comes to arranging, every American thinks of himself as a logistics expert or despairs that he is not one even as others are. He makes sure ahead of time not only that he has a hotel reservation but that it is confirmed in writing. (Even so, it is impossible to sleep in a reservation, however cheerfully worded, if the room simply has not been vacated.) He sets his radio alarm clock (but oversleeps if the power fails), keeps a spare 15-ampere fuse in the basement (but never seems to have a workable flashlight when the lights go out). We plan and then expect everything to go according to plan but sometimes are tripped up by the fact that we are human or by the fact that God is not.

Our North White Plains commuter train platform often becomes a showcase on which minor dramas of baffled expectations are enacted. The other morning, for example, the second coach instead of the third coach stopped at the spot where a clot of riders, creatures of habit, were waiting. Hardly a world crisis, but it spoiled their whole day. Though all seats were vacant, this being the point of departure, such a milling about and going to and fro to find accustomed seats!

"Where precisely will the train stop?" would seem to anyone but a commuter to be a fairly unimportant question. But it is no more so, and is indeed more answerable than, some others we dignify with theological labels, the summoning of church councils, the writing of creeds, the drawing of battle lines. Why do we *have* to know who shall roll away the stone? And as it worked out, not in a hundred years would the women who asked that question have been able to anticipate how it was in fact answered. The most they could hope for was a strong right arm. What they got was an earthquake.

We want to know everything about everything, and we want to know it right now. We want to plan—what a pathetic, human little sort of word it is, when you put it up against God! We want to know what's going on and what's going to go on, now and forevermore. I remember a dear disheveled soul I once knew who spent hours a day poring over all the "dispensational charts" she could lay her hands on, while her housework went undone. These charts pictured and timed to almost the last minute every era of man in this world and the next. She was utterly addicted to them; the merest whiff of prophecy set her off. *She* knew who was going to roll away all the stones and when and where!

Most people nowadays are not as ready as she was then to accept answers of that sort, or even to regard them as answers. For most of us, the answers are just not keeping pace with life. If we're of a questioning bent at all, we see our stockpile of questions mounting while the supply of acceptable answers is diminishing, and this bothers us even when we piously pretend to ourselves that it does not. The answer deficit runs counter to all we have been brought up on—that there is somewhere, available to us, a shining bright answer to every question. The raw fact of the matter is that there is not, at least as of now. There are simply more questions than there are answers. Sooner or later, as we contemplate the impenetrables of life or of death, we run smack up against a stone wall and we worry, "Who will roll it away for us?"

The message of faith is that worry about some things is not only unnecessary but unnerving, and this is one of them. We can—and we must—trust God to roll away the stone in his own way and time. Yet, here we are, fretting, planning, as if we had to see to it.

Among other happenings, we've put the whole resurrection experience—Christ's as it was and ours as it will be—under the microscope to try to figure it out. What kind of body did he have. Were the grave-windings left undisturbed like a cocoon from which the chrysalis had melted away? How did a "body" materialize on the inner side of a closed door, and yet partake of food? And *why* would a body need food except to sustain life as we know it? In what we call the Apostles' Creed, we solemnly avow, "I believe in the resurrection of the body . . ." when we do not even know for sure what we mean by body.

"Who shall roll us away the stone?" We will, we have been saying all too glibly. We will make sure that no question goes unanswered. We will see to it that it is all done to our complete satisfaction.

But faith declares that there are some things that God will do his way; that there are some questions he alone can answer; that there are some things we will never know ahead of time; that there are some things we don't have to know. This never-knowing will do one of two things to us. It will worry the soul out of us—or it will give us a faith that is simple enough to face death and complex enough to face life.

There is so much we don't have to know! We don't have to know who shall roll away the stone. We don't have to know all that was meant when the news was shouted, "He is risen!" We do know—by the transformation of the disciples from beaten idealists to excited realists, among other evidence—that Something happened. Often that is the most and the least we can do with an event that overwhelms us: capitalize it.

There is only one question which cannot wait for an answer: "Does God love us?" It is on this we stake our life's meaning. When we ask this one, all of creation responds, sometimes with a mightily shouted Yes! and sometimes with a still, small affirmation. In the freshness of a morning we hear it, and in the vast, lovely beauty of a sunset. In the stirring example of a life duty-driven to selflessness and even to death. In the bold, searching eyes of a baby who looks into your eyes as if he possessed the authority of heaven itself. In the myriad human evidences of love that are so common-place we never even think of them as love—the countless dishes washed, the countless paychecks earned. In the assurance that if this world does not seem kind enough, peaceful enough, courageous enough even for us, there must be Someone somewhere with enough and to spare, from whom we, imperfectly, are taking cues. And in the face of the One who better than any other took his cues.

Who shall roll us away the stone? How trivial the question seems. How trivial so many questions seem, when laid alongside the certainty that God loves us.

26) Have faith without fear

Time itself exacts a heavy toll of fear—not the time we have lived through, but the time that lies out ahead. This is what gives a special loneliness to the end of one year and the beginning of the next.

If time did not move inexorably, the chances are that a considerable slice of the populace would elect to have nothing whatever to do with an incoming year. Not that the passing year was the best of times, but we were used to it. For all the donning of silly hats, blowing of tuneless horns, throwing of paper streamers, New Year's Eve is not very gay. There is something about it like beginning a robust story, "This one will kill you . . ." and remembering you're at a funeral.

One of the reasons for this is the nature of the commodity we call time. The saying "Time is money" doesn't go far enough. Time is life. We see little pieces of us being chipped away and we see it most inescapably at the end of one year and the start of another.

A year could of course begin any time. A line down through the middle of a particular midnight is as theoretical and disembodied as a meridian on the earth's surface or the dotted boundary between Central and Mountain time. New Year's could just as well come in the middle of summer as in the middle of winter, and in the southern hemisphere it does exactly that. The ritual of New Year's, like the blowing out of candles on a birthday cake, makes visible and audible what we do not otherwise see or hear so dramatically. Unlike the birthday, this is everybody's party, and everybody knows it. Even if you're snug abed with your head under the covers, and not squealing in Times Square, you know the party's for you. And even if you're seeing out the year in church, you're where you are and those others are where they are for the same reason—you all, we all, are seeking some way to get through the confrontation to which our inventive minds have driven us. It is perhaps our most vivid reminder of death. We are ancient mariners conscripted for a journey across seas as flat and fearsome as ever they were thought to be.

And that is the other reason we are disquieted—we do not know what is ahead. Furthermore, we are fearful of what we may find. We do not like new ideas, new ways, new discoveries, new years. Ways and ideas and discoveries we can do something about or try to do something—resist the new ones, idolize the old ones—but years simply march over us. There is no defense against any one of them or against the final one. "Ready or not, here I come!" With the new comes risk and we do not like risk. Not even Christians like risks, and sometimes it seems *especially* not Christians. Despite earnest advice to the contrary, we more often than not bury the talent or the opportunity or the time or the truth entrusted to us, and we do it not because we are lazy but because we want to hang onto a sure thing.

We would rather stay with what we have just got nicely broken in—the old shoe, the old way of doing things, the old way of think-ing thoughts. Despite our feeble protestations, we chronically regard the new thing as a nuisance and very often as a threat: the new neighbor, the new neighborhood, the new employee, the new employer, the new "phase" of our children, the new tasks of the church, the newly awakened nation, the new scientific breakthrough, the new demand for this or that constitutionally guaranteed right, the new heaven, the new earth. We would much rather ring out the new and ring in the old. But that is not the way it is or can be. The old is constantly being displaced by the new and at no time does this hurt more than when the old is not a thing but a person and the person is I.

But if this is the way it is and if this is the progression in every area of life, it is a progression built into the foundations of the universe. If it is built into the universe, God built it in. And if God built it in, what are we worrying about?

God's child has a confidence that surely can tide him over times of ending and beginning: he doesn't need to fret about falling off the edge. He can never catch up to the horizon now and does he think he ever shall? Why should he fear whatever truth he may ever find, for truth is simply another name for God.

The passing of time, the coming and going, the rising and falling, the flowing and ebbing, the waxing and waning, surely deserve better than our fears.

They in fact deserve what we indeed have and for all our gay lugubriousness never quite seem to see—God the Father Almighty, the King of Creation, the Maker of time and space, standing between midnight and dawn telling his foolish children, "It is I. Be not afraid."

70 71 72 73 10 9 8 7 6 5 4 3 2 1